What people are saying about

CHOICES FOR OUR FUTURE:

"*Ocean Robbins and Sol Solomon have already energized hundreds of thousands of youth to take responsibility for their future and the future of their planet through the performances of the YES! Tour. This book goes a step further, spelling out in detail the personal life-style choices individuals can make and spreading their important message hopefully to millions of young and older people who can learn from it.*"

Roy Gamse, President, Earth Force

"*I wish I'd had this book when I was in high school. I wish everyone I knew had this book when they were in high school. If Ocean and Sol were around then, perhaps the Earth would be thriving now. Because Ocean and Sol (and people like them) are around today, perhaps there is still time.*"

Geneen Roth, author, *When Food Is Love* and *Feeding the Hungry Heart*

"Choices for Our Future *serves as a powerful reminder of how we can each help create a healthier, happier, saner world. Well-written, well-documented, and fascinating to read, I consider it one of the most important, positive, and practical books of this decade.*"

Dan Millman, author, *Way of the Peaceful Warrior*

"*Passionate and practical . . . I think it will prove to be indispensable for anyone concerned about creating a sustainable future.*"

Chris Desser, former Executive Director, Earth Day 1990

"The day Choices for Our Future *is published is my 82nd birthday. But never too late, as the bumper sticker says, to have a happy childhood, which is exactly what this book does for me.* Choices for Our Future *is well-researched and a pleasure to read."*

David Brower, Director, Earth Island Institute

*"*Choices for Our Future *is proof positive that the movement towards environmental and social restoration is present and latent within the youth of today. It is a positive and affirming vision that demonstrates that within all systems, even human systems, are the seeds for rebirth and renewal."*

Paul Hawken, author, *Growing a Business* and
The Ecology of Commerce

To Rammy,
& to a healthy world,
— Ocean Robbins

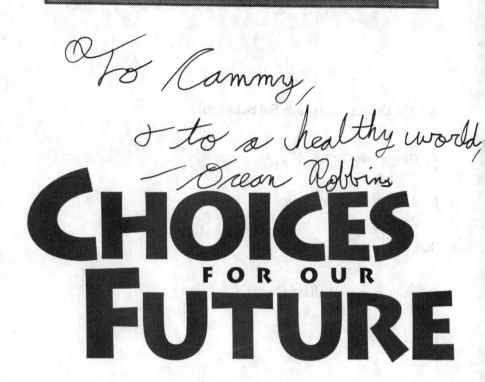

CHOICES
FOR OUR
FUTURE

OCEAN ROBBINS & SOL SOLOMON

Book Publishing Company
Summertown, Tennessee

Book Publishing Company

P.O. Box 99

Summertown, TN 38483

Cover design by Richard Curtis

ISBN   1-57067-002-1

Robbins, Ocean, 1973-
          Choices for our future : a generation rising for life on Earth /
Ocean Robbins & Sol Solomon.
                    p.   cm.
          Includes bibliographical references and index.
          ISBN 1-57067-002-1
          1. Environmentalism--Juvenile literature. 2. Environmental
policy--United States--Juvenile literature. 3. Youth--United
States--Juvenile literature. [1. Environmental protection.
2. Environmental policy. 3. Youths' writing.] I. Solomon, Sol,
1972- . II. TItle.
GE195.5.R63 1994
363.7'05--dc20   94-29060
                                                            CIP
                                                            AC

The Tree, pg. 31, used with the permission of Dana Lyons.

The Meat Eater, pg. 72, used with the permission of R. J.
Matson

Printed in the United States of America.

This book is printed with soy-based ink on paper containing as
much post-consumer material as is currently available.

Acknowledgements

In writing this book, we've been inspired, supported, and guided by countless individuals, each of whom has played a role vital to the project's success. We wish we could acknowledge them all by name. As this isn't possible, however, we acknowledge them all in our hearts.

We're grateful to John Robbins, whose editing, encouragement, advice, support, and insights have been a guiding light from start to completion. Words can hardly express the extent of our appreciation.

Thanks to Ryan Eliason, whose vision, unshakable enthusiasm, and passionate practicality not only made YES! possible, but have also touched our lives in numerous ways.

Karen Thompson nurtured and guided YES! through uncharted waters with joy, creativity, child-like gusto, and enormous charisma. Her kind heart has left a blessed mark on all of us.

Thanks to Paris Gallagher, whose dedication, courage, and friendship have meant so very much. He has always reminded us to ask why it is that people of color bear the brunt of ecological injustice.

One of the best things about being part of YES! has been getting to work with and learn from such wise, powerful, committed, and positive human beings. Each person who has joined the team has taught us much and helped to make YES! what it is today. Each of these people have also added, in ways they may never know, to making this book possible. An enormous thank you goes out to: AllahSun Eprosun, Amy Newton-McCann, Angela Kaczinsky, Chad Hoeppner, Damali Scott, Danny McCallum, David Gochenour, David Leavitt, Eden Fine Day, Eric Knapstein, G·

Quigley, Holly Pearson, Ivy Mayer, Jade Thome, Jamie Peacock, Jamie Pizzirusso, Jessica Lebowitz, Johl Chato, Johnny Sanchez, Joseph Pace, Joshua Thome, Kai McGee, Kyle Fuller, Leina Plank, Lisa Wagner, Melody Shishido, Rachel Benson, Rachel Cherry, Sam Arroyo, Skye Addis, Tammy Squires, Tauna Houghton, Veronica Sanchez, Wendy Ward, and William Leggett. May we always remember the magic.

EarthSave, and the terrific people in EarthSave, are a big part of YES!. Thanks especially to: Patricia Carney for all the advice, guidance, and love, and for reminding us so many times to look at the bigger picture; Earl Harris, who is the most youthful man alive; and to Deo Robbins, Shams Kairys, Richard Glantz, and everyone else at EarthSave for giving so generously of yourselves so many times. Thanks for giving us the freedom and independence we've needed, and for being there for us when we've needed you. You've been an incredible parent organization.

We appreciate Daryl, Marta, Tonya, and everyone else in the Cell Tech family for providing a steady and essential flow of appreciation, friendship, Super Blue-Green Algae, and dollars. Your support has meant the world to us.

Thanks to Summer Tompkins, Doug Tompkins, and everyone else at the Foundation for Deep Ecology for getting this book rolling, and for being one of YES!'s biggest supporters.

Thank you to YES!'s friends and major funders: Horst Rechelbacher and Aveda Corporation, Michael Boynton and Esprit, The Mary Reynolds Babcock Foundation, Greenpeace, Cultural Survival, Nordstrom, Peter Buckley, Jay Harris, The Fund of the Four Directions, Paul Wenner and Wholesome & Hearty Foods, The San Francisco Foundation, Richard and Rhoda Goldman Fund, The Compton Foundation, HJB Foundation, Bill Lazar, The Heart of America Foundation, Rick Ralston and Crazy Shirts, YM Magazine, Roger and Karuna Hodgson, The Phoenix family, Ani Moss, Bobby Weir, Bud Hayes, Billy Holliday, and our very first donor, Harriett Crosby. You've made it all possible.

To YES!'s local organizers, volunteers, and supporters, we have enormous cause for gratitude. We wish to express particular appreciation to Richard Curtis, Diane Danielson and YEA!, Sat Santokh Singh Khalsa, Covey Potter, Cynthia Harrington, Don Dunton, Eleanore Wasson, Karen Haim, Karl Anthony, Linda Allen, Megan Smith, Michael Klaper, Nance Escelius, Phoebe Garfield, Salima Cobb, Scott Kalechstein, the Sears family, and Tom Kruzic for all their emotional and practical support.

We are grateful to the many wise, compassionate, and committed people who have shed light on what's happening in our world today. In writing this book, we have been aided greatly by the research and insights of authors, scientists, and visionaries, and we wish to acknowledge a few who have meant particularly much to us. Thanks to *Adbusters* Magazine, *Boycott News*, Creating Our Future, David Brower, Earth Island Institute, the Earth Works Group, Friends of the Earth, Greenpeace, Helen Caldicott, Jeremy Rifkin, Jerry Mander, Joanna Macy, John Seed, Rainforest Action Network, Scott Lewis, and Worldwatch. You've all been inspirations.

Lastly, we wish to thank you, the reader. Thank you for caring. Thank you for learning. Thank you for making the choices that will bring about a healthier future.

Ocean and Sol

I slept and dreamt that life was joy;
I awoke and saw that life was service;
I acted, and behold, service was joy.

Rabindranath Tagore

Table of Contents

INTRODUCTION

We're walking through a high school at lunch time. We notice people in cliques, hanging out separately from other groups. We see "skaters" on one side of the school, "jocks" on the other, and between them are many more groups whose image is created in part by their style of clothing and music. This school is not unusual. Fads and trends dominate the social scene in most schools.

The way some people see it, there's a new fad on the rise—people wearing the "Save The Earth" T-shirts or the "Save The Dolphins" buttons—the environmentalists. At some schools, the environmental club (if there is one) is just another group to belong to—just one more trend.

Fads and trends die. They die in part because they exist on a superficial level, because people follow others instead of what's inside their hearts and souls. If the environmental movement is only a fad, then it may die just like other fads. And human life might just die with it.

The environment isn't something that only affects "environmentalists." It affects all of us and every life form on Earth. If we're going to turn the environmental crisis around, it's going to take far more than being trendy. It will need to come from our guts, our hearts, and our instincts for survival. We're going to have to go beyond superficial barriers and join forces for something we all want—a healthy future for life on Earth.

No matter who you are, no matter what color your skin, no matter how wealthy or poor your community, if you care about life, if you want clean air to breathe, uncontaminated food to eat, and safe water to drink, this book is for you. Are you a human who wants to live? That's the real definition of an environmentalist. Even though some people see the environment as a fad, it's not. It's everything that's around us and affects us. It's a reality.

CHAPTER ONE

OUR STORY

We are Sol Solomon and Ocean Robbins, ages 21 and 20. In the last six years, we have learned a great deal about the dangers to our future. As we've learned about air and water pollution, acid rain, starvation, homelessness, and deforestation, we've sometimes felt overwhelmed. We've been exposed to many depressing facts, and we've felt much despair, fear, frustration, and anger.

We wanted to do something and did what we could. Yet, it often seemed that hardly any other young people felt as deeply as we did about responding to the threats facing our future. Many youth seemed only apathetic and frustrated—unable to put out the effort to create positive change.

We weren't willing to silently stand by and let life on Earth suffer, as we saw so many of our peers doing. We had to respond.

In the spring of 1990, at the ages of 17 and 16, we were two of the founding members of an organization called Youth for Environmental Sanity, or YES!. We raised money. We organized. We educated ourselves further. We worked and worked, and then we worked some more. Eventually, we went on a national speaking tour, talking to junior high and high school assemblies about environmental issues. We talked about the environmental crisis and about choices. We talked about what young people could do to make a difference. Along with the other four YES! Tour participants, we raised $90,000 and spoke to 80,000 students in our first year.

The response to our presentations was amazing. After every assembly, young people came up to us, deeply moved, to express their appreciation and support. Sometimes, people told us the experience had changed their life in positive ways. We felt that we were striking a chord deep in the heart of America's youth.

After we left a school, young people began creatively acting for constructive change. One group of students got their school district to ban styrofoam. A second got their student store to sell only recycled paper products, while a third began organizing school campus clean-ups. Some got their cafeterias to start composting, while others organized regional school speaking tours. The numbers of young people in school environmental clubs grew exponentially. The movement for youth empowerment and environmental sanity was on.

By 1994, YES! had 14 members between the ages of 17 and 24, representing nine states, Canada, and Mexico. We were reaching 150,000 students annually, conducting return visits and training workshops at many schools, and were organizing at least four youth action training camps each summer. The organization had gone international, with tours starting in Australia and New Zealand and camps coming up in Singapore and Taiwan.

We weren't doing badly for an organization that was, and always has been, completely youth run.

Ocean Robbins:

I was born in a one-room log cabin on a little island off the western coast of Canada. My family was miles from our nearest neighbors, surrounded by the trees, the deer, the rain, and the silence. We drank good water, breathed good air, and ate wholesome vegetarian food.

I spent my first years playing as much with the forest as with other children. I knew every tree, every rock, and every season. I grew up taking for granted what many people no longer have: things like clean air, clean water, time with my mom and dad, and a healthy environment.

I grew up far away from the world's problems, happily playing and learning, living on a little island, with a few toys and a few friends and no television or movies. I grew up poor, but I grew up feeling rich.

Sol Solomon:

I grew up in the city.

From my earliest years, I watched television, went to movies, and attended baseball games with my dad. I did eat meat. My father lived in San Francisco, and my mother lived across the bay in Berkeley, which left me going back and forth, with two parents and two lives. Nature was a place I occasionally visited and enjoyed, but I always returned to my home in the city.

When I was thirteen, I moved with my mom, step-father, and little brother to Orange County, California. I moved from the multi-cultural birthplace of the hippie movement to a region that was practically a national monument to right-wing, conservative thinking. This move catapulted me into a phase of rebellion. I got into the "heavy metal scene," became a graffiti artist, and did my share of drugs. Because I had long hair and a different shade of skin than the mostly Caucasian people around me, I experienced prejudice frequently. My family saw that Orange County wasn't working for us, so we moved to Los Angeles.

Ocean:

As the years went by, I started to learn about pain and suffering in the world. My family moved to Santa Cruz, California, and I began to realize that not everyone had the opportunities and the joys that I had taken for granted. I often felt overwhelmed by social and ecological problems. Sometimes I wondered how long I would have a safe world in which to live. While I cared deeply about

17

the environment, I often felt isolated from my friends, as if I was somehow weird or different for being concerned. Most of my friends didn't seem to think about things like world peace or the environment. They seemed more interested in shopping malls and television.

In 1989, I attended a summer camp at which I met other young people who wanted to make the world a better place. Joining with others who felt as I did, I found my fears about global problems beginning to be replaced with a new possibility: the joy of acting for what I believed. Meeting with other youth who shared my concerns and my desire to make a positive difference was a turning point in my life. For the first time, I felt a sense of community with other people my own age, one of whom was a young man named Ryan Eliason. Together Ryan and I conceived the vision that was later going to turn into the YES! Tour.

The first step was to find other young people who shared our dream and would join us in making it a reality. My dad, John Robbins, had become a leader in the health and environmental movements, had founded a non-profit organization called EarthSave, and was doing a great deal of public speaking. I contacted Ivy Mayer, 16, and Rachel Benson, 18, who had come to his talks, and soon the four of us were speaking to high school audiences in the San Francisco Bay Area about the environment. At first, we called ourselves the Creating Our Future Tour. We received such positive responses that we knew our work had to grow. EarthSave decided to take us on as a project, and with non-profit status and a small amount of organizational backing, we began the YES! Tour.

The next summer, Ryan and I were both facilitators at the same summer camp at which we had met. We were looking for the right people to join our project.

Sol:

It was in Los Angeles that I first encountered environmental problems head-on. I'll never forget those blistering hot, smoggy days. Or the times when I would be cooling off in the ocean and notice trash and the occasional piece of "human excrement" floating past. I used to think that the ocean was a toilet bowl that hadn't been flushed. Warring gangs and crack addiction infested my neighborhood. Every day I was bombarded by the injustices of our society and shocked by the enormous gap between the "haves" and the "have nots." On the bus ride to school, I used to watch wealthy people passing and ignoring others who had no homes. I felt claustrophobic and overwhelmed by the chaos of the city. I had to get away.

I discovered a place in the Santa Monica Mountains where I found freedom and joy. Almost every weekend, I went there to climb rocks, go hiking, and savor natural beauty. These hikes became something of a lifeline to me, providing me with the opportunity to experience something profound and special. One day, while sitting in these mountains, I noticed an apartment complex being built down below. I was struck with a combination of sadness and inspiration, sadness because I saw that my favorite place in the world might soon be destroyed, inspiration because I felt the voice of nature speaking to me, inviting me to be a vehicle for its survival. I looked at the city off in the distance, and I knew that I had a mission: to help this world.

My quest to change the world led me to start an environmental club at my high school and later to attend a summer camp in northern California.

Ocean:

When I first met Sol at camp, I didn't know what to think. He looked like an obnoxious dude who thought he was cool and wanted everyone else to think it too. He was wearing a black baseball hat backwards, blasting the Red Hot Chili Peppers on his stereo, and cussing profusely. At the time, I was looking for people who might be good members of the YES! team. Sol wasn't on my list of possibilities.

Sol:

I thought Ocean must have been from Mars or something. The guy had a constant smile on his face as if the whole world was some fairy land. He listened to new age music, always wore clothes that gave some environmental message, and acted like he thought he was a saint. I figured he'd lived his whole life sheltered from the real world. But he was funny, entertaining, friendly, worked well with the group, and for those reasons I almost liked him.

Ocean:

As the camp progressed, my initial judgments of Sol began to fade. He took an active role at the camp and was clearly comfortable in a leadership role. Towards the end of the camp, he led an exercise about sexism that opened my eyes to issues about which I had previously been ignorant. This exercise had a powerful impact on me and the entire camp, making room for deep understanding and healing to take place. As I began to look beyond his personality, I came to see a profound depth and commitment that inspired me. I was gradually and surprisingly beginning to respect this person who came from such a different background and yet had so much to offer.

Sol:

I still thought Ocean was pretty strange. I was impressed by his knowledge of environmental facts, but sometimes he reminded me of a walking encyclopedia. Even though I thought he was odd, somehow he symbolized the next step in my life. On the camp's last day, all of the participants were hugging good-bye and exchanging addresses as new friends saw each other off. Ocean and his friend Ryan Eliason took me aside and presented me with an information packet on the tour they wanted to create, asking me if I wanted to join. I said, "Yes," and Ocean responded, "That's the name of the organization." Even though we were different, I could see our common purpose, and I was eager for us to start working together. So began one of the most humbling and learning-filled times of my life.

When I moved to Santa Cruz a month later, I met up with Ocean and Ryan. They had been joined by Karen Thompson, who had heard Ocean's dad speak in Vancouver. The four of us were soon joined by a few other young people. We began our crusade for environmental sanity by working massive hours to turn our common vision into a reality. To me, YES! has always been a mission, a cause, and a labor of love, never just a job to do. I gave my all. Work only stopped when the day's work was done, not when 5 P.M. arrived or when it was a weekend.

As time progressed, I began to feel a great deal of respect for Ocean. He knew how to get things done. He was a committed, professional, and productive office worker who seemed to generate incredible results in fund-raising and almost everything else he did. He worked hard, yet he never sacrificed his commitment to enjoying life and keeping a positive, up-beat attitude. Words could never express how much I've learned from the gift of Ocean's friendship. The person I once thought

21

was sheltered from the world has helped me to be more effective in my mission to change it.

Ocean and Sol:

As YES! developed and grew, we were excited and inspired. We were successfully accomplishing our goals, creating enormous positive change and doing something that had never been done; at the same time, we were ordinary young people working together on behalf of what we believed, and we were accomplishing extraordinary things. We felt our success was a living statement that by making positive and responsible choices, young people can create a better future. YES! had become a powerful example of people from diverse backgrounds joining forces and making dreams become realities.

None of this came easily. There was an enormous amount of office work to do, money to raise, and decisions to make. YES!'s participants always seemed to have strong personalities and the desire to be leaders. Learning to value the diverse perspectives in our group, work as a team, and streamline our efforts was a challenging process.

We didn't want to repeat the power struggles that are so common in our society. We wanted to blaze a new path. We wanted to value each another and the process, as much as the end result, and at the same time, to be efficient and successful. Believing with Gandhi that "the means are to the ends as the seed is to the tree," we chose to make our lives examples of the values we hold dear.

Ryan, Karen, and the two of us were the beginnings of a team that became an organization that has worked to change the world. We were later joined by many other youth who helped to carry the dream forward. Between 1990 and 1994, there were a total of 44 of us in YES!. We spoke to more than 475,000 students in person across the continent, facilitated workshops and camps for thousands of youth, and reached another 100 million people through local and national television, radio, newspapers, and magazines.

Through our involvement in the youth environmental movement, we've learned about the common problems and possibilities encountered by youth working together. We've learned about getting along with people, handling money, having successful meetings, speaking in public, and the power that comes from working with a diverse group to accomplish worthy ideals.

In helping to create YES!, we've learned about one of the most important tools any of us has to create a positive future: the ability to choose.

The future of life on Earth, and of our own lives, is powerfully affected by every choice we make. And yet, so many of us still don't understand what we are creating by how we live; we don't grasp the impact of our actions. If as members of the human race we can learn how we affect the world and learn how to make wise choices for our future, we will turn the environmental crisis around. It is this hope that has launched the book you now hold in your hands.

CHAPTER TWO

LIFE ON EARTH

Many of us live in a cement-covered world, rarely in contact with the Earth that lies beneath the concrete. We can become caught up in the clothes we wear, the cars we drive, and the money we have—so caught up that we may forget the foundation of our existence: planet Earth.

Our planet provides everything we need to survive. We have food to eat, forests to explore, and mountains to climb. We have air to breathe, water to drink, and land on which to live. This world houses a great variety of plants, animals, insects, birds, trees, and people, each with their own unique role to play in the harmonious interdependence of life on Earth. The Earth is a generous host, a beautiful, blue-green gem, rich with diversity and wonder.

Join us now on a journey. Imagine that we're hiking in the mountains. Ahead, we can hear the sound of rabbits dashing through the bushes. Above, two red-tailed hawks glide gracefully through the clear blue sky. We sit on a rock at the bottom of a hillside, marveling at the stillness that fills the air. With our every breath, we savor the scent of flowers and sage.

A large autumn leaf drops from overhead, swaying from side to side with the air's currents and finally landing near our feet. Picking it up, we notice the scurrying of a small colony of black ants.

Indeed, life is abundant.

Seeing a formation of rocks above, we start to climb, looking forward to exploring the majestic peak. We reach out with our hands, grabbing the largest rock crevices as we slowly make our way upwards. The sun is going down, but its warm glow still fills the air with heat and light.

Now, we have almost reached the summit, and our arms tremble as we struggle to complete the final stage of our climb. Pulling ourselves to a kneeling position on what feels like the top of the world, we catch our balance and slowly rise to a standing position. Mountains and valleys stretch as far as we can see.

Gazing off into the distance, we imagine what life must have been like for the natives of this land a few centuries ago. Throughout their entire lives, they lived with the magical presence of these mountains and valleys. Their culture respected the Earth and all its creatures. For the native people who once roamed this land, this wasn't "the natural world." This was "the world."

Basking in the magnificent view before us, we slowly turn around and are saddened by what we see. It's a major city, or what we can view of it through the thick, brown haze that enshrouds this sprawling metropolis. Turning to our side, we look at the natural beauty around us and then back to the city off in the distance, suffocating in a thick blanket of polluted air.

We picture the small weeds and blades of grass that victoriously edge their way through cracks in the asphalt. We think of the trees, growing in patches of dirt where cigarette butts and trash cover their polluted soil. We think of the city's birds, who never land in deep forest nor fly over vast expanses of open wilderness. Instead, they fly from stop signs to telephone wires and back again.

This city is enormous; it seems to stretch almost forever. What was once a small town has grown to take over the fragile wilderness that previously surrounded it. At the edge of the city, we notice tractors and cement mixers engulfing ever more nature in the constant expansion of the city's concrete jungle.

This city is growing like a cancer, spreading across the land, gobbling up the Earth. Looking at the development projects on the closest edge of the city, we wonder how long it will be before they swallow up the mountains in which we've been hiking.

We think of the people, bustling about, hurrying from place to place, caught up in the city's frantic pace. We picture the billboards, neon lights, tall buildings, shopping malls, and the constant flow of cars, buses, and trucks. We imagine the sounds of car engines, horns, and police sirens, of road and building construction, of human voices talking and shouting, of televisions and radios, and of airplanes. We think of the smells that fill the air: automobile exhaust, cigarettes, restaurants, factories, chemicals, perfumes, plastics, and paints. The senses of the people in this city are under constant assault.

For many of these people, the closest they will ever come to nature will be watching it on television or walking through zoos and city parks. Can they know what silence sounds like? Can these people understand nature? If a hawk flew over their heads, would they notice it? Have these people grown so used to toxic air and polluted water that they think it is normal? Can they have any feeling for the nature being sacrificed for their way of life? Do they know what is happening to their air, water, and forests?

THE BREATH OF LIFE

Take a moment to notice the air filling and emptying your lungs as you breathe.

As you continue breathing, imagine a small goldfish swimming in a fish bowl. The water around it is clean and pure. Just as we depend on our air, this fish depends on its water. Suppose a drop of poison falls into the fish bowl. With its every breath, the goldfish takes some of the poison into its body, eventually becoming so polluted that it dies.

Now, notice the air you're breathing. If someone were to put enough poison in it, what would happen to you?

Through the air you breathe, you are interconnected with every living being on Earth. In every breath you take, there are molecules that have been cycling through the atmosphere of this planet for billions of years. There may be molecules that were once inhaled by a tyrannosaurus rex, by Michael Jordan, or by Mother Theresa. And the Earth's plants and trees provide a fresh dose of oxygen to our every breath.

Have you ever smelled the fumes that come from buses? Many of us can hold our breath when we are exposed to a bus's exhaust, waiting for the toxic cloud to disperse. But what if the air was always that polluted?

For some people, it almost is. Breathing Mexico City's contaminated air is as damaging as smoking two packs of cigarettes every day.[1] In Tokyo, vending machines sell clean oxygen at street corners. In 1988, 40,000 Czechoslovakian students wore respirators on their way to school to shield them from air pollution.[2] On 75 days of that year, southern Californians were told that children should stay indoors.[3] Children brought up in these polluted areas suffer reductions of 10-15% in lung capacity for the rest of their lives.[4]

In the U.S., some 150 million people breathe air that the Environmental Protection Agency considers unhealthy.[5] Air pollution leads to the death of 120,000 Americans every year.[6] It costs the United States more than $40 billion in health care annually.[7]

This level of air pollution isn't natural. When we burn fossil fuels in our cars and factories, and when we burn our planet's forests, we release carbon dioxide and poisonous chemicals into our atmosphere. Cars, factories, and burning forests all have one driving force behind them: the activities of people. Whether we're hiking in the mountains or driving downtown, we are always interconnected with the life force of the Earth that provides our every breath. As you will see in the chapters soon to come, if we make wise choices, our air can become clean, pure, and life-giving.

WATER, WATER EVERYWHERE, BUT NOT A CLEAN DROP TO DRINK

Seen from space, vast blue oceans and fluffy white clouds cover most of the Earth's surface. Massive glaciers caress the top and bottom of this beautiful, watery planet. A closer look at the Earth's land reveals fresh, trickling streams, cascading waterfalls, rushing rivers, and lakes of every size and kind. Everywhere, water is evaporating, forming clouds, and then raining back down to the Earth again. This continuous cycle provides nourishment and pleasure to most of the world. Water can bring life to a desert, quench our thirst, and cool us off on a hot day. All the Earth's inhabitants depend on this precious resource.

Just like the air we breathe, the water our bodies use intimately connects us with each other and our entire planet. Every drop of water has been cycling through the world for billions of years. Water from the ocean evaporates, collects into the clouds above, sweeps around the planet, becomes rain, and falls to Earth. Eventually the water finds its way into a stream. A thirsty deer may drink water from this stream and later deposit it at the base of an apple tree. The water sinks into the soil, enters the tree's roots, travels up the trunk, goes through the branches, and finally provides a ripening apple with life-giving liquid. Eventually, this apple may nourish a human being.

While humans can survive for weeks without food, we can live for only a few days without drinking the water that flows through us, lubricating our joints, and keeping our bodies cool. Ninety-nine percent of the molecules in our bodies are water molecules.[8] Without clean water, we die.

Three-quarters of the world's surface is water, but 99% of that is unusable to us, because it is found in oceans and glaciers. Only 1% of the Earth's water is usable.[9] A small portion of the water we use comes from rivers, streams, and lakes. Most of it is ground water from cracks and crevices beneath the Earth's surface.

Around the world, drinking water is being contaminated by agricultural pesticides and fertilizers, animal waste, mining operations, leaking garbage dumps, industrial and household chemicals, acid rain, sewage, and oil or chemical spills from factories. If we do not learn to care for the small percentage of the Earth's water that is usable, we may come to appreciate this natural treasure the hard way.

"In Oklahoma, oil has leaked to a nearby creek, where it forms a sticky layer on the water's surface and coats the banks. The oil's toxicity has rendered the water uninhabitable to most forms of life, and it is no longer fit for animals to drink."

J.W. Maurits la Riviere, *Scientific American*

Contaminants can be found in every body of water in the world, including our tap water. The Environmental Protection Agency has found more than 700 pollutants in U.S. drinking water.[10]

In 1982, the tap water in Charlotte Mock's neighborhood of Albuquerque turned oily and metallic tasting. Charlotte and her neighbors found little black flecks floating in the dishwater and toilet bowls, noting that, *"whatever is in that water, it eats the chrome off the bathroom fixtures."* After some research, Charlotte and her neighbors learned that their water was completely unsafe for human consumption and that 18,000 people were, nevertheless, drinking it.[11]

In Woburn, Massachusetts, 19 children died because they drank water from their community's polluted wells.[12]

Many cities add chlorine and up to 60 other chemicals to their water to make it "safe" for drinking.[13] Unfortunately, many of these chemicals have foul tastes and odors, color the water, and are suspected of causing cancer and other diseases.

Some people have decided that the solution to our water problems is to drink bottled water. Although bottled water costs 900 times more money than tap water, U.S. residents purchased 1.7 billion gallons of it in 1989.[14]

While buying bottled water may be a good idea, it is far from the solution to this problem. Many people can't afford it, and animals don't even have the choice. As you will see later in this book, we can each do much to save the clean water we have and to keep it from becoming contaminated. Through the choices we make with our food, energy, and trash, we can help to purify the waters of the Earth.

ROOTING FOR LIFE

What would the world be like if we suddenly lost all our trees? There would be no more wood with which to build our houses or to burn for heat. In a short time, our oxygen supply would sharply decrease, and breathing would become difficult if not impossible. Gases like carbon dioxide that otherwise would have been absorbed by trees would build up, eventually causing almost all oxygen-based life on Earth to die. All over the world, there would be rampant soil erosion, for with no trees to hold dirt in place and store the moisture, rain would cause floods that would wash away the soil. Rivers and streams would become highways of run-away dirt; lakes and seas would become pools of mud.

In the year 900 A.D., forests covered approximately 40% of the land on Earth. Today, they cover less than 20% of our planet's land mass, and that percentage is shrinking fast.[15] In the U.S., deforestation occurs at a still more frightening rate. Ninety-five percent of our first-growth forests have been cut down in the last

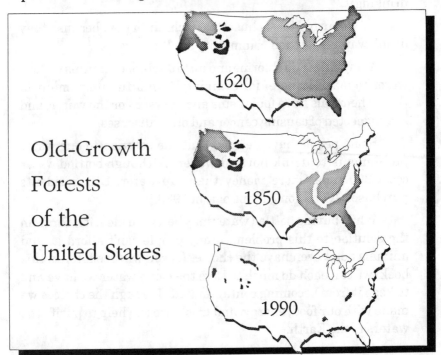

Old-Growth
Forests
of the
United States

1620

1850

1990

century.[16] Out of all our remaining first-growth forest, more than 80% is slated for logging.[17]

Looking out through the eyes of a tree, the environmental songwriter Dana Lyons tells us,

> *"There's a river flowing near me,*
>   *and I've watched that river change and grow.*
> *For eight hundred years I have lived here,*
>   *through the wind, the fire, and the snow.*
> *I see salmon return every summer,*
>   *and I watch young owls learn to fly.*
> *I have felt the claws of the grizzly,*
>   *and I have heard the lone wolf's cry.*
> *I have seen great glaciers melting,*
>   *and I've met lightning eye to eye.*
> *But now I hear bulldozers coming,*
>   *and I know that I am soon to die.*
> *But who will house the owl?*
> *And who will hold that river shore?*
> *And who will take refuge in my shadow*
>   *when my shadow falls no more?"*
>
> *The Tree,* a song by Dana Lyons

Trees are crucial to our survival. You don't have to be a "tree hugger" to see their importance. But they are under attack from the mentality that looks at an ancient forest and instead of valuing the trees as a crucial part of our life-support system, starts calculating board feet and thinks only of short-term profits. They are in jeopardy largely because of a mentality that sees trees merely as a product to sell or something that's in the way of mining for minerals or grazing land for cattle, a mentality that doesn't realize how dependent we are upon this critical natural resource.

We have choices to make. Might it be possible to permanently save all of our remaining first-growth forests, to plant as many trees as possible, and to grow "tree farms" for things that require wood? Might we make our paper from other materials and eat in a more forest-friendly way? The choice is ours.

There is much each of us can do to save our forests. We can come to cherish and care for our air, water, and land. We can begin to realize their importance in our lives. We can learn to protect them.

CHAPTER THREE

TURNING THE EARTH INTO PRODUCTS

While the human-made world in which most of us live can seem separate from the Earth, it's not. No matter how many roads we pave or how tall our buildings become, we will always have a connection with the Earth that supports us.

There are four particular kinds of choices we make in the "human world" that dramatically affect the ability of the Earth to thrive and sustain us. They are:

- *The material objects we make and consume.* Every product we use affects the soil, the air, the water, and all the other life-support systems upon which our lives depend.

- *The food we eat.* We would not be able to live without the Earth's food that provides us with the nutrition and energy we need to survive. Every time we eat a meal or purchase a food product, we are influencing our future in dramatic ways.

- *The energy that fuels our society.* No stereo, light bulb, heater, or naval destroyer would be possible without the energy that comes from the sun and the Earth. Every time we turn on the switch and burn energy, we affect our climate, air quality, and health.

+ *Who we are and how we relate to the world.* As humans, we are at the root of the problems our world is facing and of the solutions that are emerging. In every moment, we create the future with our attitudes and actions.

What would happen if we became aware of how the material objects we purchase and use affect the future of all life?

Those of us who live in human-made environments consciously experience only a few life forms. Mostly there are other humans—a lot of them. Then there are cats, dogs, ants, pigeons, rows of planted trees and flowers, trimmed bushes, mowed lawns, and a few other kinds of living things. But this can not compare to the enormous variety of life in untouched wilderness areas.

For most of us, there is no longer an abundance of life forms in our experience. Instead, there is an abundance of material objects. The diversity most of us know is the incredible variety of human-made things, like lamps, pots, cars, houses, roads, dishes, sneakers, disposable packages, stop signs, cameras, and other manufactured items.

The materials from which these things are made were all once a part of the Earth. Parts of our cars are made of metals. The plastic bags in which we put our sandwiches come from oil. Both oil and the minerals used to create metal once rested deep beneath the Earth's surface. The cotton in the clothes that we wear grew out of the Earth's soil. So did the trees that make our desks, paper, and houses, and the food that we eat. Our glass is made from sand. Even toxic chemicals, styrofoam cups, and paved roads are made from materials that were once harmonious participants in the web of life.

The elements of nature are being transformed into lifeless objects for us to use and consume. We are turning the Earth into products that are bought and sold.

DON'T BUY THE HYPE

"Our enormously productive economy ... demands that we make consumption our way of life, that we convert the buying and use of goods into rituals, that we seek our spiritual satisfaction, our ego satisfaction, in consumption ... We need things consumed, burned up, worn out, replaced, and discarded at an ever increasing rate."

Victor Lebow, retailing analyst

The U.S. advertising industry spends nearly $500 on you every year.[18] Every other person in North America gets the same attention. From our earliest years, we have been bombarded with dozens of commercial messages every day. A typical high school student's brain absorbs about 14 chocolate and candy ads, 3 fast-food ads, and 4 sugary snack and soft drink ads before dinnertime.[19] Corporations advertise because it leads to more customers and more products sold. Today, Americans drink more soda pop than water.[20] Even though cigarette smoking stinks and kills, it's on the rise among young people because of the huge blitz of advertising aimed at the youth market.[21]

... Once an addict, always a customer ...

The advertisements we see can make us feel that we need to buy things in order to be happy. Even the names of many of the products we buy portray feelings we want to have. We can clean with "Joy," eat "Life," wear "Hope," smoke "Lucky," drive "Spirit," and splash on "Love."

"Human happiness is just too important a thing to trivialize like that, to consumerize like that. Happiness is something we create together, it's something we give each other, it's something we live. It's not something that can be bought or sold."

John Robbins, author
Diet For A New America

35

Even if we know that happiness is not something we can buy, commercial messages continue to manipulate us, driving us to buy more, to have more, to be in style, and to value image and convenience. We are not encouraged to think about the long-term consequences of our actions. Meanwhile, huge amounts of our planet's resources are being gobbled up, and masses of trash are piling ever higher.

With every product that we buy and dispose of, we consume our future.

The U.S. and Canada, with five percent of the world's population, use a third of the Earth's natural resources.[22] We're using up our natural resources faster than they can be replenished. After we take them from the Earth, what do we give back?

GARBAGE

"The waste generated annually in the United States would fill a convoy of 10-ton garbage trucks 145,000 miles long— over half the way from Earth to the moon."

The Greenhouse Crisis Foundation,
101 Ways To Help Heal The Earth

Most of us buy dozens of products every month, use them, and throw them "away." We rarely think about where our garbage goes.

Eighty-five percent of U.S. garbage ends up in landfills, which are massive dumps where trash piles up until they become full. Then they are closed and new ones must be found. All over the U.S., these dumps are filling, leaving many states with no space for their garbage. Often trash travels huge distances, sometimes even thousands of miles, to an available resting place.

In a forest, there is a continuous "recycling" of plants that die and decompose into dirt, with new plants growing in that dirt. Unfortunately, our garbage doesn't work the same way. Inorganic materials, which make up much of our garbage, won't break down for a long time. In landfills, the garbage is so tightly compressed under its own weight that it never gets exposed to significant amounts of sunlight, water, or the tiny creatures (like microbes, worms, and bugs) that help organic materials to decompose. The result is that even things like newspapers, which you would expect to break down quickly, can stay perfectly readable for decades.[23]

Landfills are dangerous. They contain many toxic chemicals that anyone in their right mind would not choose to drink. Garbage juice is anything but appetizing. But today, many people who drink water from their tap can experience small amounts of this unique beverage.

> *"Rain trickles down through the mass of garbage, picking up toxic heavy metals and other contaminants which then may leach through the bottom of the landfill and into the ground water."*
>
> Susan Hassol and Beth Richman,
> *Recycling*, The Windstar Foundation

In 1986, the New York Department of Environmental Conservation estimated that half of the state's 420 landfills were polluting ground water.[24]

> *"We offered to settle for one dollar if the court would close the landfill. The court refused to close the landfill. They admitted that the landfill did damage the aquifer. It did damage my well. It must have poisoned my children. But we collected nothing . . . We dreamed there was justice in the American courts. We got wiped out (by the rich companies that dumped their waste in the landfill)."*
>
> Frank Kale, a New Jersey homeowner
> whose well was contaminated[25]

Landfills don't seem to be an adequate answer to our waste disposal problem, yet that's where most of our garbage goes when we throw it "away."

HEY, WHY DON'T WE BURN IT?

As our dumps fill up and our garbage continues to roll in, a new option for disposal is on the rise: incineration. Incinerators now burn over 15% of our trash, and their usage is increasing fast, so rapidly in fact, that they deserve some serious attention.[26] Incinerators are popular because they have some advantages. But a deeper look removes some of the glamour.

Incinerators are sometimes called "waste-to-energy" plants, because they turn some of the heat from the burning garbage into electricity—but not much. In total, about 0.2% of the U.S.'s electricity comes from incinerators.[27]

Another attractive feature about these burners is that the waste is reduced to ashes, taking up only 30% of its original volume.[28] Unfortunately, the toxic ash created by incinerators contains some of the most poisonous substances ever known. Most of it could be classified as hazardous waste, but it's not.[29] Why? Because hazardous waste has to be disposed of in special ways that are safer than simple burial but cost more money. In the early 1990s, the incinerator industry persuaded the Environmental Protection Agency (EPA) to create a special category for their toxic ash. This category made incinerated ashes cheaper to dispose of than if they were classified as hazardous waste. It saved money, but the real price was people's health.[30]

According to the EPA, more than half of the nation's 5.3 million tons of annually produced ash goes to landfills.[31] And the rest?

"As for the fate of the remaining 47 percent, it's unknown."
Bill Breen
Garbage Magazine, March /April, 1991

Handled without proper safeguards, some of the ash finds its way out of storage and into our soil and water. From there, it's a short jump into our food and our drinking water. Remember, these substances are so toxic that in large enough amounts they can kill.

"It's ironic. The reason cities started building incinerators in the first place is because town dumps are filling up and polluting water supplies. Now they're dumping the same toxics that were in the garbage to start with, plus a whole new set created in the furnaces. The difference is that some of those toxics are more concentrated and more soluble in water than they were in their original state."

Jim Valette, Greenpeace toxics campaigner

POISONING THE AIR

Some incineration centers pre-sort garbage before burning it to recycle metals, to compost organic materials, and sometimes to remove plastics (which produce toxic gases when burned). But most incinerators are the "mass burn" type that produce a toxic mixture of pollutants, including sulfur dioxide, nitrogen oxides, and hydrogen chloride. These gases give people lung problems, are toxic to plants, corrode metals, and contribute to acid rain.[32]

Heavy metal particles coming out in the smoke at the top of incinerators enter the air that we breath. These particles include lead, mercury, cadmium, and arsenic, all of which can cause cancer, birth defects, and many other serious health problems.[33]

The Semass incinerator in Massachusetts emits 2,000 tons of toxic chemicals into the atmosphere every year.[34] Unfortunately, this figure is not unusual.

"A nation neck deep in garbage, garbage that is rich in recoverable resources, is rushing to burn its refuse. The burning precludes recovery, releases toxic wastes into the air and leaves a poisonous pile of black ash, which is buried in the ground—certainly a form of madness, by any standards."

Judy Christrup
Greenpeace Magazine, May-June, 1988

TOXIC RACISM

Because of their toxic emissions, incinerators are not wanted in many communities. It is no accident that incinerators are usually built in areas inhabited by people of lower income, people who may not have the time or the money to oppose them.

A recent report prepared for the state of California on where to build incinerators was titled, "Political Difficulties Facing Plant Siting." [35] The report says that when choosing sites for building incinerators, it's best to look for communities with the following traits:

- High school education or less
- High unemployment
- Blue-collar workers
- Lower income communities
- Minority groups

The communities that use incinerators often have high Afro-American, Latino, and other minority populations. Three out of every five Afro-Americans and Latinos in the U.S. have a toxic site in their community.[36] This is environmental racism, plain and simple.

Some communities stop incineration plants from coming to town. Navajo natives in Dilcon, Arizona, defeated plans for a toxic incinerator and landfill on their reservation.

> "I believe that they had the idea that because we're a minority, we're looked at as not being able to defend ourselves. I'm glad that we got involved in this and opposed this construction."
> James Paddock, *The Navajo Nation*, Dilcon, Arizona

Unfortunately, many people in communities targeted for incinerators haven't succeeded in keeping their communities safe. McFarland, California, is the home of Marta Salinas and her family. Her town is also home to a toxic incinerator.

> *"When we first moved to this area, we started noticing that our neighbors were suffering some types of skin rashes, and we realized that we all have the same health problems ... My little girl says to me sometimes, 'Mom, I know I'm gonna die someday, but I do have a wish. My next birthday wish is I want clean water and dirt. And if I die of cancer, I wanna go be with my kittens, how they've all been dying ...' She says, 'Is there anybody who cares about us Mom?' And I tell her, yes, there are, but they just don't know what's happening."*
>
> Marta Salinas

Another McFarland resident is Angie Irmiter. Her daughter has mysterious and painful bumps on her neck. Some of Angie's doctors say her daughter has cancer. This has caused her to take action, starting Mothers Involved In Fighting Toxics to do what she can to clean up her community and rid it of the toxic incinerators and landfills that are poisoning her and the people she knows.

> *"You don't want to think it's cancer. But these thoughts keep going through your mind because of everything you've seen around you in your community and your friends dying and children being so sick, and I guess now it's hit home. It's one of my kids."*
>
> Angie Irmiter

Millions of people live in fear for themselves and their families because of incinerators. But the damage goes beyond hurting and even killing people. There is another price that we pay.

Through our taxes and garbage fees, we pay big money for the incineration "service." An incinerator, with a lifetime of about 20 years, costs hundreds of millions of dollars.[37] Garbage burning is a major business, and it brings powerful companies a great deal of money, enough money that they can afford to persuade, intimidate, and otherwise convince local governments that incineration is the best alternative. Sold as the modern way to handle trash, incinerators are actually an effective way to waste our land, air, water, health, and money.

DON'T RECYCLE!

The companies that run incinerators are paid for every ton of garbage they burn, and if they don't burn up to capacity, their profits drop. As recycling grows in popularity, many of these companies are scared—because some communities might not have enough garbage for them to burn. So they often make deals with the local authorities. The government must provide them with a minimum amount of garbage per day or pay a penalty.[38] This leaves communities that have built incinerators with a financial distaste for recycling.

In 1989, the county of Warren, New Jersey, adopted a recycling program that was so successful the county didn't have enough trash for its local incineration plant. As a result, the plant's builder and operator charged the county $2.5 million in penalties.[39] The Semass plant in Massachusetts (which burns 1,900 tons of garbage every day) is responsible for making recycling almost non-existent in the 32 communities it "serves."[40]

Recycling garbage is safer and healthier than incineration or landfills, and it's cheaper too. Nationwide, it costs about $100 a ton to incinerate garbage, $90 per ton to put it in a landfill, and $40 a ton to recycle it.[41] Ironically, in 1987, *Newsday* found that state governments spent 39 times as much money on incineration as on recycling programs.[42]

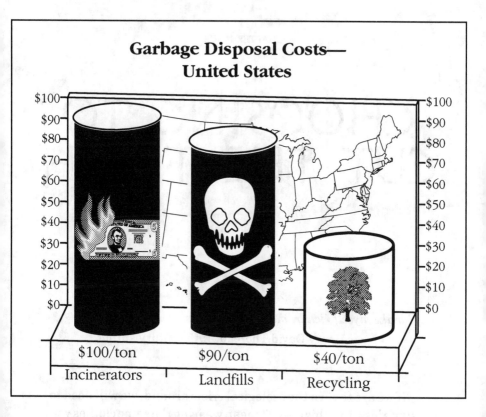

Garbage Disposal Costs—
United States

$100/ton — Incinerators
$90/ton — Landfills
$40/ton — Recycling

Today, every time we throw something in the trash, we may be adding to the mass of incinerators that have been or will be built. With this simple action, we add to the fear and pain of all those who will become ill or whose loved ones will suffer from the ash and smoke incinerators produce.

We need to produce less trash. Wise choices can enable us to cut down on our consumption and on our trash production tremendously, without any compromise in our quality of life. Some shifts in our life-styles may at first seem inconvenient. But it can be even less convenient to drink garbage juice and blacken our lungs with toxic incinerator emissions.

CHAPTER FOUR

CHOOSING TO CUT THE TRASH

"I make myself rich by making my wants few."
Henry David Thoreau, 19th century author

If we are to turn the ecological crisis around, we will need to consume less. But this doesn't mean wearing the same clothes you wore in preschool and sharing your toothbrush with your three closest neighbors. It's really a question of being efficient. Efficiency means not wasting so many of our resources on products that won't actually make our lives any better.

DISPOSING OF THE WORLD

It seems as if we have disposable everything. We can buy disposable razors, cameras, napkins, "silverware," dishes, pens, rags, and contact lenses, all wrapped in throw-away packages. For the sake of "convenience," our society turns the Earth's resources into disposable you-name-its that end up in landfills or incinerators, contaminating our air and water. This is ridiculous when you consider that there are usually alternatives to disposables that are of better quality and cheaper in the long run.

Think of the disposable products that you've used in the last week. Were there alternatives to disposables in any of those situations?

We can take our own reusable dishware to restaurants or potlucks that use disposables. This may seem inconvenient, but it sets a powerful example. It can even be a good idea to keep reusable dishes at school, at work, or in a car, so that we're always prepared. We could be eating off our favorite dishware, while everyone else eats off their flimsy, throw-away piece of bleached paper or styrofoam.

Most of us are familiar with the experience of standing at the check-out counter and being asked, "Paper or plastic?" At such times, we may face a dilemma, with neither of the options sounding too appealing. Plastic comes from petroleum and will be toxic in landfills or incinerators, while paper comes from trees, of which too few remain. We may weigh the pros and cons, and try to choose the lesser of the two evils. But there's a far better solution: reusable canvas shopping bags. Do you have one? They're much stronger and easier to carry than paper or plastic bags, and of course they last much longer.

The average, disposably-diapered baby uses a ton of disposable diapers every year.[43] Once a disposable diaper enters a landfill, it will stay there for 500 years before it breaks down.

> *"Over a billion trees are used to make disposable diapers every year."*
> The Earth Works Group,
> *50 Simple Things You Can Do To Save The Earth*

While disposable diapers are useful for hours, cloth diapers are useful for years.[44] In most areas, cloth diapers are also less expensive than disposables, even if the family uses a diaper service. To top it off, babies who wear cloth diapers get diaper rash five times less often than those who wear disposables.[45]

Does this mean no one should ever use a disposable diaper? There might be situations (such as traveling) where disposable diapers are a major convenience. But once we understand the facts, cloth diapers become the primary choice.

(For more information on local diaper services, see National Association of Diaper Services, page 161)

BUYING IN BULK

After we buy a product in a store, we usually take it home, rip it open, and throw away the packaging, without even thinking that we are making a contribution to our garbage pile-up. But packaging materials now account for half of our municipal waste.[46]

"If 10% of Americans purchased products with less plastic packaging just 10% of the time, we could eliminate some 144 million pounds of plastic from our landfills, reduce industrial pollution, and send a message to manufacturers that we're serious about alternatives."

The Earth Works Group,
50 Simple Things You Can Do To Save The Earth

When we cut down on packaging, we can save money too. How? By shopping at natural food stores or supermarkets that offer items like beans, nuts, and grains in "bag-it-yourself" bulk bins.

Many people don't shop at natural food stores because they think organically grown, natural food is too costly. But most natural food stores have bulk bins, which more than makes up for the higher prices of healthier food. As you can see in the chart on the next page, buying in bulk can be significantly less costly than buying the same product already packaged.

Staff of Life is a large natural food store in Santa Cruz, California. Down the street from it is Safeway, a large supermarket. The chart shows a price comparison of the two stores for a random assortment of items. At Staff of Life, all the items listed are in bulk, which as you will see, dramatically brings down the price. Safeway only sells them in packages, so the prices are adjusted according to a system of pints and pounds to provide a valid comparison. In some cases, the items are sold for a variety of prices, in which case the whole range is given, from the least costly to the most expensive. An * indicates that the item is grown organically (without pesticides or chemical fertilizers).

Saving Money, Health, and The Planet[47]

Item	Prices from Safeway	Prices from Staff of Life
Almonds	$7.76/lb	*$3.25/lb
Brown Rice	86¢/lb	40¢/lb-*79¢/lb
Buckwheat	$2.70/lb	*$2.28/lb
Oats	$1.56/lb	*79¢/lb
Olive Oil	$2.82-$6.71/pint	$2.90/pint
Pinto Beans	99¢/lb	89¢/lb
Raisins	$1.70-$3.41/lb	*$1.59/lb
Sesame Oil	$7.59/pint	$3.47 pint
Soy Sauce	$1.92-$4.32/pint	$1.17/pint
Tahini (sesame butter)	$2.70/lb	*$2.28/lb

CHOOSING TO RECYCLE

There are other ways to cut the trash. An ambitious recycling program would go a long way towards saving natural resources, energy, and money, towards creating jobs, and towards cutting disposal costs and problems. It would be a big improvement over the garbage can and a big step forward for our future.

What can you recycle?—aluminum, glass, tin, plastic, organic waste (compost), paper, and more.

DON"T CAN ALUMINUM

Of all the recyclable items, an aluminum can is the easiest to make into a new one. It melts at a relatively low temperature and saves a great deal of mining.

Recycling one 12-ounce aluminum can saves an amount of energy equal to six ounces of gasoline, enough to power an efficient (40 MPG) car for two miles.[48] In 1988, the aluminum cans that Americans recycled saved enough energy to power New York City's residential needs for six months.[49] Compared to trashing it, recycling aluminum also cuts air pollution by 95%.

> "Since 1981, over half of the 300 billion beverage cans sold in the United States have been returned for recycling; the average can that is returned is re-melted and back on the supermarket shelf in six weeks."
>
> Jeffrey Hollender
> How To Make The World A Better Place

What's amazing is that we're only recycling half of our aluminum cans. In fact, we throw away enough aluminum to rebuild our entire commercial air fleet every three months.[50]

THROUGH THE (RECYCLED) LOOKING GLASS

Recycling glass reduces air pollution by 20% and water pollution by 50%, compared with trashing it.[51] Every time you recycle an average glass bottle that would have been trashed, you save enough energy to light a 100 watt bulb for four hours.[52]

Although recycling glass costs jobs in the container production industry, it creates more jobs in the recycling industry. Michigan reports that passing a "bottle" bill (creating a program designed to promote recycling) led to a net increase of 4,500 new jobs. In New York, a similar bill led to an increase of 5,000 full-time jobs.[53]

Even better than recycling glass is reusing jars and bottles. When we recycle glass, it often has to be trucked great distances to a factory where it can be melted for re-shaping. Because glass is heavy and dense, both the trucking and the melting require large amounts of energy.

TIN CANS

Recycling tin cans reduces related energy use by 74%, air pollution by 85%, solid waste by 95%, and water pollution by 76% compared to trashing them.[54] That sounds great, doesn't it? But we only recycle 5% of our tin cans! Let's change that. If your recycling center takes them, terrific. If not, maybe they need a little convincing from you.

RECYCLED PLASTIC

In the last few decades, plastic use in North America has risen dramatically. There are good reasons why it's so popular—it's lightweight, waterproof, strong, and durable. But plastics are made from petroleum, and most don't decompose for a long time.

Humans dump more than 45,000 tons of plastic trash into the world's oceans every year, killing up to one million seabirds and

100,000 marine mammals annually.[55] "Degradable" plastics may be a slight improvement, but not much. Because they only break down into smaller pieces upon extended contact with sunlight, they provide virtually no advantage inside a landfill or incinerator.

A spokesperson for Mobil Chemical Company, manufacturer of Hefty® "degradable" trash bags, admitted the real reason "degradable" bags are promoted as being so environmentally friendly,

> *"(Degradable bags) are not the answer to landfill crowding or littering . . . Degradability is just a marketing tool . . . We're talking out of both sides of our mouths when we want to sell bags. I don't think the average customer knows what degradability means. Customers don't care if it solves the solid waste problem. It makes them feel good."[56]*

In 1987, the U.S. used almost one billion barrels of petroleum just to manufacture plastics.[57] That's enough to meet U.S. demand for imported oil for five months.[58] We can save that oil and the disposal problems of plastic by reducing our use of it, reusing it, and when possible, by recycling it.

Many recycling centers are starting to take plastic. The complication is that there are many different types of plastic in use. Fortunately, there are a few kinds of plastic that are used more than all the others, and they are the ones that are most easily recyclable. It's important to separate plastics so they can be recycled in the appropriate bin. If you look carefully on the bottom of any plastic container, you'll probably find a recycling symbol (♳) inside of which is a number. If you live in an area where plastic recycling by numbers is available, match this number with the numbers on the recycling bin.

COMPOST IS GREAT STUFF

Imagine walking through a forest. If you were to scoop up a layer of leaves under a tree, you would see composting in action.

The top layer is leaves, twigs, and needles. Below them are last year's leaves, twigs, and needles—which are in the process of being transformed into rich, crumbly soil.

If you were to visit this forest 100 years later, you might see the same tree, having now fallen to the ground and been converted into a home for billions of microorganisms, bugs, and earthworms. These little critters have done such a good job, along with the heat of the sun, water from the clouds, and oxygen from the forest, that a beautiful young tree is now proudly growing from the soft, nutrient-rich soil that has developed from what once was the old tree. In nature, every living thing eventually gets composted, breaking down into dirt and nourishing the new things that will grow in the place of old ones.

By setting up a compost pile, you can bring this wonderful, natural process into your backyard, bringing yourself a little more into contact with nature.

Thirty percent of U.S. household trash is yard clippings and kitchen scraps.[59] Sending these materials to landfills or incinerators is ridiculous, because they are incredibly valuable resources. When composted, they become the healthiest and richest type of natural fertilizer. In only five to ten minutes per week, a person can "recycle" his/her organic waste by composting it and putting it back on the land.

Fortunately, more and more people compost their kitchen wastes and yard clippings. One way we know this is by measuring the number of compost bins sold each year in the U.S. In 1988, only 35,000 people bought compost bins. In 1992, more then 700,000 people bought them.[60] More than three million American homes are now composting, and the number is growing daily.[61]

(To learn more about composting, read the wonderful book, *Backyard Composting*.
You can get a copy in bookstores, or see the ordering information on page 163.)

THE CHOICE FOR RECYCLED PAPER

"We are presently cutting down 100 billion trees annually to produce paper products! However, even this vast number of trees is not enough to satisfy our ever-growing hunger for paper. The multinational pulp and paper industry is presently undergoing unprecedented expansion. New mills are being built in many developing regions, such as Latin America, as well as in Canada and Australia, to take advantage of the last remaining virgin forests in the world."

> Renate Kroesa, *The Greenpeace Guide To Paper*, 1990

If we would simply recycle our paper and use recycled paper, we could cut our municipal waste almost in half.[62] We could save most of the water, energy, pollutants, air pollution, and all the billions of trees that go into making paper out of forests.[63] Recycling paper creates five times more jobs, and it even saves money.[64] It makes sense! The Institute of Scrap Recycling Industries says paper recycling in the U.S. is now saving over 200 million trees per year, even though recycling efforts are nowhere near what they could be.

"If you recycled your own copy of the New York Times *(or a newspaper of similar size) every day for a year, you'd save the equivalent of 4 trees, 15 pounds of air pollutants from being pumped into the atmosphere, 2,200 gallons of water, and enough energy to power a 100 watt light bulb for 152 days."*

> Jeffrey Hollender,
> *How To Make The World A Better Place*

Most of us have the habit of throwing used paper in the garbage can. Recycling paper means learning a new habit—separating our discarded paper into piles: newspaper, colored paper, and white paper.

We can even reuse paper. If you have paper that's only used on one side, the other side is still good. You can save it and take it to a local printing company who will bind it into a new pad or into several smaller pads.

You can also reuse envelopes, boxes, and packing materials you receive in the mail. It's great to get a rubber stamp made that says something like, "This envelope was reused to save trees." That way you can set a positive example for others, and no one will think you were just being sloppy.

THE CHOICE TO USE RECYCLED PRODUCTS

It's wonderful that many people are recycling, but just recycling by itself isn't enough. We need to complete the cycle by using recycled products. Not enough people and companies use recycled paper. This makes recycled paper more expensive, which makes people less likely to choose it, which makes the cost higher, and so it goes. Sometimes paper just sits in huge warehouses for extended periods of time, waiting to be recycled. If it isn't used, it may even be dumped into landfills or incinerators. We need to start using recycled paper in our homes, schools, and at work.

We can work to get local businesses, newspapers, and printing companies to use recycled paper. If any of them uses alternative paper, we can write them a letter of appreciation for caring about our future or thank them in person.

We can demand that our local school administrations use recycled paper. If they say the photocopy machine can't handle it, get them to try another source or to use paper made of 50% recycled materials. We can also demand that school student stores sell only recycled paper goods.

Schools should prepare us for the future. Don't you think they could help make sure there is a future?

IS RECYCLED PAPER RECYCLED?

"Much so-called 'recycled' paper is bogus, and consumers will have to get much more serious about recycling if it is to have its intended effects."

Ed Ayres
Worldwatch, September /October, 1992

"Recycled paper" isn't necessarily recycled—at least not as we generally understand the term. The important distinction is between paper made from "pre-consumer" and "post-consumer" waste, both of which cost slightly more than new paper. The Environmental Protection Agency has given in to lobbying from the paper industry and dictated that paper made only from pre-consumer waste can be labeled "recycled." Pre-consumer waste has fibers that the paper industry decides would have been wasted if they weren't "recycled."[65] This paper is sometimes just a high-priced sham. Many companies in the paper industry are delighted with this rule, because it enables them to charge more money for lower quality paper, all the while looking like environmentalists.[66]

"It would be possible for all the paper used by federal, state, and local agencies throughout the United States to be '100 percent recycled' according to the EPA's definition—and not reduce the flow of garbage by one ounce, or the cutting of trees by one twig."

Ed Ayres
Worldwatch, September /October, 1992

Post-consumer recycled paper is what "recycled paper" implies itself to be. It is used paper that has been recycled into more paper.

You may be able to get post-consumer recycled paper at a local stationary or office supplies store. You can definitely get it, in numerous forms, through the mail from both of these companies:

◆ Conservatree Paper Company wholesales a complete line of all or partly post-consumer recycled paper products for businesses or schools. It sells computer paper, high-speed copier paper, offset paper, linen text, and envelopes. Conservatree also provides valuable information on recycling, paper, and other environmental issues. Call (415) 433-1000 for a copy of the company's price list and sample book, or write: 10 Lombard St., Suite 250, San Francisco, CA 94111.

◆ Real Recycled sells hundreds of things made from 100% post-consumer recycled paper, including stationary, cards, pads, envelopes, gift-wrap, copier paper, computer paper, and a full range of office paper supplies. To get a copy of their catalog, call (800) 233-5335; or write to 1541 Adrian Rd., Burlingame, CA 94010-2107.

CHAPTER FIVE

POWER TO THE BUYER

No matter how much or little we cut our consumptive habits, most of us will, of course, need to buy certain products. With every thing we do buy, we can have great power, the power that comes from choosing to support or avoid specific products or companies. Through buying in accordance with our beliefs, we can help create a better world.

Who gives some corporations the power and the money to pollute our environment? Who gives certain other corporations the signal to be socially responsible, ecologically friendly, and to be leaders in making a better world? We do, by buying their products. Every dollar we spend is a vote. We're voting for the store we buy the product from and for the company that makes it. We're saying, *"I support you. Here's some money, now make another of these just the way you made this one, to replace the one I just bought."* Our dollars could be supporting environmentally responsible projects. But they also could be supporting toxic waste incinerators or pesticide-related deaths in the grape fields of California.

"If companies don't do the right thing, I will . . . by not buying their products."

Brett Hilsabeck, high school student

Organized boycotts are changing the way companies do business and the way consumers think about shopping. There have been hundreds of successful boycotts all over the globe, and many of them have profoundly affected our world.

RACISM ON THE BUSES

Let's go back to Montgomery, Alabama, in 1955. This is the South and there are laws designed to discriminate against Afro-Americans. One day, an Afro-American woman named Rosa Parks gets onto a crowded bus. According to the law, she must sit in the back of the bus, and if a Caucasian person wants her seat, she is expected to move. But on this particular day, she is hot, tired, and fed up with the injustices that oppress her. When a Caucasian man asks for her seat, Rosa Parks doesn't budge. Later that day she is put in jail, but no bars could possibly contain the passion and motivation for change that her choice inspired.

In the following months, tens of thousands of people boycott the racist bus system in Montgomery. Many of these people have to walk for hours every day to get to work or school. But they are willing to endure the struggle, because they know the importance of the movement they have begun.

After the bus companies of Montgomery lost much of their revenue, they were forced to change their rules, allowing people of any race to sit wherever they wanted. This victory helped catalyze the civil rights movement, as Martin Luther King, Jr., and millions of others began to lead America towards social justice.

DOLPHINS IN PERIL

Another momentous boycott saved the lives of countless dolphins. Dolphins are amazing creatures with an extraordinary level of compassion, intelligence, and love of life. They have, many times, been known to help people stranded at sea.

In June of 1971, Yvonne Vladislavich was on a yacht that exploded and sank in the Indian Ocean. She was thrown into a shark-infested, violent sea with no land in site. Things didn't look good for Yvonne, but she was saved by three dolphins. One held Yvonne up, while the other two swam in circles around her, guarding her from the sharks across two hundred miles of open sea. Eventually, she climbed onto a marker, from which she was soon rescued.[67]

Dolphins are remarkably kind creatures. They have been more than generous to humans, but many of the people they've encountered have been anything but generous to them. In the 1970s, commercial tuna fleets all over the world began using driftnets, some of which were thirty miles long.[68] Trailing off the sides of ships, they would hang in the water like enormous curtains of death, capturing and killing everything that came in their path, including dolphins.

Mother dolphins nurse their young for more than a year, creating a strong bond between mother and child. Dolphins several years old have been known to seek out their mothers when they become frightened. Most of these animals care so much about one another that they will not abandon an injured dolphin, even if it costs them their own life.[69]

When tuna nets catch infant dolphins, mother dolphins will go to extraordinary lengths to join their doomed young. Once in the nets, mothers will huddle with their offspring, singing to them as they die together. In 1987, 16,000 dolphins were killed by the tuna industry; most of these were dolphin children and their mothers.[70] Their dead bodies provided no use to humans, but their fate was sealed because they swam near tuna.

In 1988, Earth Island Institute and several other organizations, outraged by the large-scale slaughtering of innocent dolphins for American tuna, launched a boycott of all tuna caught using methods harmful to dolphins. Soon this boycott gathered national attention and was joined by tens of thousands of people. Many restaurants and entire school districts took tuna off their menus unless it was caught using dolphin-friendly methods. Awareness of this issue spread fast, and as Earth Day 1990 approached, the boycott's momentum continued to grow.

On April 12, 1990, Heinz, owner of Star-Kist, held a press conference in which they announced an end to their part in the dolphin slaughter. Nearly a year later, Bumblebee joined them. Several companies still kill dolphins, but that may change soon as dominos continue to fall. When buyers express their outrage, even multi-billion dollar companies like Heinz are forced to respond.

BRINGING GOOD THINGS TO DEATH

If you were to visit certain towns in eastern Washington state, you might notice unusual feelings in the air. You might feel the almost tangible sense of resentment, frustration, and fear that have terrorized many of these communities. There's a neighborhood in one of these towns that has come to be called by a new name: The Death Mile. Twenty-seven out of twenty-eight families in this neighborhood have experienced life-threatening health problems.[71]

In 1949, June Casey, a sophomore at Whitman College in Washington State, was 19 years old and full of hope. But she lived near the Hanford Nuclear Reservation—where General Electric and the U.S. army manufactured plutonium for weapons. One Christmas, June visited her parents in Oregon and was shocked to find her hair falling out. It never grew back. She later developed a case of hypothyroidism that her doctor described as "the most extreme case" he had ever encountered. It wasn't until years later that June Casey learned the Hanford Nuclear Reservation had caused her health problems.

Unfortunately, June is only one of thousands of people who have become ill or even died as a result of this one plutonium factory.[72] More then 50 Nagasaki-sized bombs could be manufactured from the waste that has leaked out of Hanford's underground tanks.[73]

In the 1980s, General Electric was the largest manufacturer of parts for nuclear weapons.[74] Their factories, located across the U.S., became notorious for dangerous working conditions and nuclear radiation that frequently contaminated nearby communities.[75]

"What GE (General Electric) does is . . . mislead the American public. They pollute the Earth. They dump toxic waste. They irradiate their workers, and they are one of the largest producers of nuclear weapons in the world."

Greg Erickson, owner, More-4 Supermarkets, 1991[76]

Remember how incineration companies convince local governments to burn trash and how paper companies persuaded the EPA to loosen the laws about what can be called "recycled" paper? Well, GE used the same tactics on a much bigger scale. In the 1980s, GE had the largest Washington, D.C., lobbying office of any company in the world, with more than 150 employees.[77] The company's lobbying efforts helped convince our government that 26,000 nuclear war-heads (enough to extinguish all life on Earth many times over) wasn't enough.[78]

"It is the companies like GE that push Congress into building more weapons than we need."

Gene La Rocque, former rear admiral, and now Director of the Center for Defense Information

In 1984, INFACT, an international grassroots coalition of concerned people, launched a boycott that sent ripples of consumer action around the world. INFACT called for a boycott of GE products until the company stopped producing nuclear weapons. INFACT also produced a documentary video called *Deadly Deception* which exposed GE's activities. *Deadly Deception* later won an Academy Award for Best Documentary-Short in 1991. Across North America, young people led the way in the spread of awareness about the boycott. Students at more than 330 schools organized campaigns to educate people in their communities on the issue.

By 1992, the GE boycott had grown to include more than four million people and 450 organizations—costing GE hundreds of millions of dollars.[79] Thousands of letters from concerned citizens streamed into GE's headquarters, imploring the company to pull out of the nuclear weapons industry. Eventually, public pressure overwhelmed one of the largest companies in the world. On November 23, 1992, GE decided to get rid of its aerospace division, which had previously been responsible for the manufacture of parts for many nuclear weapons.

"The success of this grassroots campaign shows that ordinary people can move a trans-national corporation and make a real difference."

Elaine Lamy, Executive Director
INFACT

Today there are hundreds of active boycotts taking place. Every person who joins a boycott adds to its power and effectiveness.

THE OZONE LAYER CRISIS

"Stratospheric ozone depletion threatens us with enhanced ultraviolet radiation at the Earth's surface, which can be damaging or lethal to many life forms."

Excerpted from a warning signed by 1,500 scientists, including 104 Nobel Prize winners

The United Nations Environment Program (UNEP) reports that ozone layer depletion is already damaging people's immune systems and causing cataracts, skin cancer, phytoplankton loss, and crop damage.[80] UNEP also reports that as ozone layer depletion continues to grow, these problems will also grow.

Many North American scientists have been looking to Australia as a model of what may be happening to our continent in the next few decades because the ozone layer is thinning there more rapidly. The model is far from encouraging. In Australia, the sun burns people even during brief walks outside. There are daily ozone reports in the news, and on the worst days, people are warned not to go outside for more than 15 minutes at a time. Rates of skin cancer and blindness are slowly becoming epidemic.

> *"Almost every Australian over the age of 75 has skin cancer."*
>
> Dr. Helen Caldicott, Australian pediatrician

On the Australian continent, the sun has become something to fear. People are told to hide from its warm rays, and for a good reason. The ultraviolet radiation that is blasting through a wiped-out ozone layer is hitting Australia hard. And it's not just people who are suffering. Plants and animals are also struggling to tolerate the increased ultraviolet radiation. Agricultural productivity is down, and if the ozone layer thinning continues much longer, some people wonder how much food production will be possible.

The problems of ozone layer thinning have already spread beyond Australia.

> *"Increased ultraviolet radiation has induced blindness in 12-15 million people and has impaired the vision of 18-30 million others. Every 1% decrease in the ozone layer causes a 4-6% increase in the number of skin cancer cases around the world."*
>
> Global Youth Forum
> The UNCED Conference, 1992

In 1993, NASA reported that the ozone layer over the United States was 18% thinner than it had been a decade earlier.[81] Meanwhile, Canadian Dermatological Associations have publicly warned that tanning is no longer safe, and that babies under one year old should not be exposed to direct sunlight at all.[82] The problem is expected to cause hundreds of thousands of skin cancer deaths in the next century.

> *"Already, skin cancers have tripled in Australia, and farmers in southern Chili, alerted by widespread blind-*

ness among rabbits and other animals, religiously don
dark glasses before working their fields. Ten years from
now, will even those of us in more moderate climes be
covering from the sun like ghastly nocturnal creatures in
a science fiction nightmare?"

Mark Herstgaard,
San Francisco Examiner "Image"
June 7, 1992

THE WORLD CAN'T WAIT FOR DU PONT

The hole in the ozone layer has a name on it, and it's a familiar one to most of us: Du Pont.

Du Pont has produced the majority of the world's CFCs (the primary ozone-destroying gas). Du Pont has finally agreed to phase out CFCs, but is replacing them with HCFCs, which *also* destroy the ozone layer, and with HFCs, which are a potent greenhouse gas.[83] There is a good deal of debating among scientists as to whether or not HCFCs are as bad as CFCs, but the fact is that even if they aren't as bad, they still destroy our ozone layer.[84] Essentially, the "H" that's been added on to the "CFC" just stands for "Hype." It takes at least 15 years for ozone-destroying chemicals to reach the ozone layer, and they remain active there, destroying ozone for decades. So it is imperative that we take action to immediately halt the production of CFCs and other chemicals that destroy the ozone layer.

Our ozone layer is thinning. Lives are being lost. The crisis is deepening.

In 1991, Greenpeace, Ozone Action, and many other organizations launched a national boycott of Du Pont products (along with Seagrams and Tropicana, both of whom are closely affiliated to Du Pont). The boycott will continue until Du Pont stops producing *any* chemicals that destroy the ozone layer and begins research into how the company can undo the damage that has already been done. Du Pont has the opportunity to cease being one of the worst villains of our times and become a company with the courage to include the future of life on Earth, along with profits, in its agenda.

Let's help Du Pont make the shift. Successful boycotts depend on letters to the company involved from active boycotters, explaining the reasons behind the boycott.

(See page 165 for Du Pont's address)

When you write to Du Pont, expect them to send you a fancy packet of information that makes them sound like environmental saints. The truth is that they have a massive public relations department whose purpose is to make them look good. Consider yourself warned in advance: Don't buy the hype.

(To find out more about the ozone layer and how to help it, see Ozone Action, page 160.)

THE PENAN MEET MITSUBISHI

The Penan people in the Sarawak rainforests of Malaysia have lived in harmony with their environment for the last fifty thousand years. They are an extraordinarily peaceful culture, and their language has no word for "war." The Penan dwell throughout the forest, leaving virtually no trace of their presence. For thousands of years, the Penan have enjoyed clean streams and boundless forests rich with a diversity of foods and medicines.

The Penan are one of several cultures who live in Sarawak's rainforest. All of these people are now endangered. Their rainforest is being logged faster than any other forest on Earth. The destruction goes on 24 hours a day, seven days a week.[85] At first the Penan, along with the other rainforest peoples, retreated deeper into the jungle as the deforestation emerged, but soon they had nowhere to run. The streams became brown with the topsoil that washed off the land that had been their forest. With every passing month, new roads made way for the ongoing destruction of these rainforest peoples' home. Of the 7,600 Penan remaining in 1993, 75% had been forcibly relocated into government camps where they lived an alien life-style with polluted water and inadequate food and medicine.[86] One of the oldest cultures on Earth is being destroyed.

All for what?

"A full 80 percent of Sarawak's forests are loaded into ships bound for Japan, destined to become cheap furniture, packing crates, and plywood for concrete forms."

National Boycott News, Winter 1992-93

The people of Sarawak's rainforest have tried everything in their power to save their home from destruction. They have organized blockades and inspired millions of people to write letters on their behalf.[87] But the destruction won't stop until we, the consumers, stop supporting the companies who are responsible for the logging. In 1988, the Rainforest Action Network joined JATAN (a Japanese environmental coalition) in calling for an international boycott of Mitsubishi, saying that this company is one of the largest destroyers of Sarawak's rainforest and the world's other rainforests.

(For the Rainforest Action Network address, see page 160 and to write letters expressing your concern to Mitsubishi Corporation, see page 165.)

BABIES FOR PROFIT

Now imagine that you're in a small town in the less "developed" part of the world. You could be in Asia, Africa, or Latin America, and the situation would be similar. There is little electricity or clean water, and there are few toilets. Children play in a stream where sewage pollutes the water. Nearby, mothers care for their young.

One of these mothers feeds her baby from a bottle filled with water and infant formula. She has just returned from the hospital where she gave birth to a beautiful baby. At the hospital, a nurse gave this mother a free sample of Nestlé's infant formula. She loves her newborn baby and wants the little one to be healthy like the babies she sees on the infant formula billboards and cans. She doesn't have any heat to boil the water as the can suggests, and the only water she can mix with the powdered formula is polluted. But she feels confident that the formula will still be the best thing for her baby, because the Nestlé representatives told her so. She mixes it up and feeds it to the infant.

A short while later, the sample gets used up. The mother goes to the store to buy more, and finds out that a two weeks' supply costs more money than her husband makes in a week. As it is they can barely get by, so she decides that she will have to breast-feed her baby, because she cannot afford the formula. The mother goes home and discovers that her breast milk has dried up. She doesn't realize that if she had breast-fed from the beginning, she would have a continuous flow of ample, safe, and nutritious milk for her baby. Nestlé strategically supplied her with a free sample that would last just long enough that her breast milk would have dried up. Now her baby is crying from hunger, and she is forced to save up money to buy Nestlé's infant formula. By eating only once a day, she and her husband are barely able to save enough money to supply their baby with a watered-down version of the formula that is making Nestlé millions.[88]

An infant's body is sensitive and fragile and cannot handle formula made with polluted water. The artificial milk becomes a daily dose of disease and malnutrition. The baby develops diarrhea and eventually is unable to digest any of the formula its parents have worked so hard to provide. A few months later, the couple has lost a dear member of their family. The little one died of what is technically classified as "bottle baby disease." Every year, more than 1,500,000 babies die from this disease.[89]

Most of these babies would have lived healthy lives if they had been breast-fed. They are victims of a clever but ruthless marketing strategy by the Nestlé Corporation and other infant formula manufacturers. By giving away free samples of their infant formulas to hospitals in "third world" countries, these companies get mother's breast milk to run dry, hooking them on the product. Even though breast milk is far healthier than bottled formulas, the infant formula companies trick mothers all over the "third world" into killing the babies they love. If these mothers fed their babies exclusively with breast milk, the death rate among these infants would drop by 95%.[90]

Between 1977 and 1984, an international coalition of health care, church, and community groups staged a massive boycott of all Nestlé products. In 1984, Nestlé agreed to stop donating free samples of their formulas to hospitals. The boycott was declared a victory, but it was short-lived. Nestlé and several infant formula makers, including American Home Products, are at it again. Together, these corporations are responsible for the death of millions of babies each year.[91] Closer to home, these companies are now donating free infant formula samples to inner city hospitals in the U.S. The devastating impact of the infant formula scam is being felt all over the world.

Action for Corporate Accountability is spearheading the boycott of Nestlé, American Home Products (AHP), and the companies they own. Nestlé owns Carnation, and AHP owns Advil.

(If you want to contact Action for Corporate Account-ability, see page 159. To write letters telling Nestlé and American Home Products what you think, see their addresses on page 165.)

THE POWER OF "BUYCOTTING"

The power of the buyer doesn't stop with protesting companies that are doing things we don't like. It also comes from choosing to support companies that are doing good things. Many corporations want to make the world a better place.

Some use recycled materials for their paper, stationary, catalogs, and packaging. Others have environmental departments that answer questions and coordinate environmental affairs. Some companies pay their employees to volunteer their time for non-profit organizations, others choose not to test on animals, and others use organic ingredients in their products. There are companies that put on film festivals and training seminars to educate their staff about the environment. Many donate generously to good causes.

Based on our research, we recommend the following companies: Aveda, The Body Shop, Cell Tech, Eden Foods, Esprit, Imagine Foods, Kellogg's, Patagonia, and Wholesome & Hearty Foods. Many other companies are doing good things too.

> (Want to find out about the environmental, animal testing, minority and woman hiring, and charitable contributions records of the companies you are likely to buy from? Order *Students Shopping for a Better World* from the address on page 161.)

GREENWASHED

"The smart (companies) are going green, the dumb ones are not, and the foolish ones are pretending."
David Kreutz, *The Globe and Mail*
Toronto, Canada

According to the Institute of International Research, 77% of all American consumers say their buying choices are affected by a company's reputation on environmental issues. This is leading many companies to spend millions of dollars on improving their environmental image.

Unfortunately, some of this money goes more towards public relations than making the world a better place. In April of 1990, a two-page advertisement with a drawing of the Earth and a caption that said "HANDLE WITH CARE" appeared in numerous magazines across the U.S. Twenty-two of the nation's 50 most polluting chemical producers were sponsors of that ad.[92] Of course, the companies who sponsored the ad included their names along with the "environmental" message. The whole thing was a hoax that made it seem that they were ecologically responsible.

"Don't believe the hype."
Public Enemy, rap band

When we see an ad that makes a company appear environmentally conscious, we might be wise to think twice before unquestioningly believing it. In 1985, Chevron conceived the "People Do" ad series and was soon spending many millions of dollars on this campaign to improve its environmental image.[93]

One of Chevron's magazine ads depicts a beautiful fox with a coyote off in the background silhouetted by the full moon. The ad is called "The little fox and the coyote," and it says,

> "Across the twilight of a California desert, a kit fox hears the deadly footfalls of a coyote. Caught in the dangerous open, she can streak for safety to a curious mound on the edge of an oil field. People who work there, consulting with wildlife experts, built it specially for her.
>
> "So now she can squeeze through a pipe just big enough for her and into a cozy den that's designed to keep her snug and safe.
>
> "Do people think of things like this just to help an endangered species make it through the night? People Do."

This ad makes Chevron look like an environmental hero for saving the kit fox. But they're not exactly telling the whole story. The San Joaquin kit foxes live in the Lost Hills area of Kern County, California, next to one of Chevron's drilling sites. These foxes have become endangered largely because of companies like Chevron who have destroyed the foxes' habitats.[94] Chevron pretends to be helping to save this species, but according to Earth Island Institute, the truth is that the company has only built seven dens for kit foxes, and they are usually vacant.[95]

> "To my knowledge, no one has ever seen a coyote chase a kit fox into a den."
>
> A kit fox expert who requested anonymity [96]

The cost to build and install Chevron's seven kit fox dens totaled about $7,000.[97] The company then spent millions of dollars creating ads and plastering them in magazines around the world, trying to convince us that Chevron was helping to save animals.

The truth is that Chevron is one of the biggest polluters in the U.S. In 1987, they were fined $145 million because of violations and environmental degradation for which they were responsible.[98]

Do people really think they can destroy our environment and get away with making themselves look like ecological heroes? People do.

OUR FUTURE, OUR CHOICE

Every time we buy, use, or dispose of something, we are making choices that affect all life on Earth. The forests, animals, dolphins, infants, and other people with whom we share this planet depend on us to take a stand for our future. If we choose wisely, our water, air, and land will be cleaner and safer for generations to come, and we will have helped humanity to move closer to ecological and social responsibility.

THE MEAT-EATER

Chapter Six

CHOW NO COW

Think about what you normally eat for breakfast, lunch, and dinner. Many of your meals may include foods that damage or help your health and our environment in ways you might never have guessed. The food you eat three times every day can be a powerful choice for the future.

Some of us are touchy around this subject, because what we put in our mouths is a personal issue. But given the tremendous impact of your food choices, you have a right to know what's happening behind the scenes. Let's start with a look at the global food supply.

MORE PEOPLE...

Every year, 92 million more people join the human race—that's like adding another Mexico to the world.[99] Every one of those people needs a home, heat, transportation, food, and water, and every one produces waste.

In the last 40 years, the human population has doubled. During that time, the rise of human numbers has forced farmers to dramatically increase crop production.[100] Today, population is still rising, but the world's food production isn't.[101]

PLUS LESS FOOD...

Pressured to feed billions of new people, farmers have adapted methods that are not sustainable and have eroded the foundation of our food production: topsoil. Without topsoil, our land can't grow food. It takes nature an average of 600 years to create one inch of this precious resource.[102]

Two hundred years ago, most of America's croplands had at least 21 inches of topsoil. Today, most of them are down to about six inches of this natural treasure, and the rate of its loss is accelerating.[103] Globally, we lose 761 tons of topsoil every second.[104] Some of our farmland has already lost so much topsoil that it can no longer grow food; it has turned into desert.

EQUALS STARVATION

"In the last ten seconds . . . three children died from the effects of malnutrition somewhere in the world. No statistic can express what it's like to see even one child die that way . . . to see a mother sitting hour after hour, leaning her child's body against her own . . . to watch the small, feeble head movements that expend all the energy a youngster has left . . . to see the panic in a dying tot's eyes . . . and then to know in a moment that life is gone."

UNICEF

Most of us are familiar with television images that show staving children with bloated bellies and emaciated bodies. These horrifying pictures make many of us feel uncomfortable. And if we want, we can conveniently switch the channel or turn off the television. But whether or not we're willing to look at it, the suffering continues. And whether or not we know it, many of us contribute to world hunger. How? Through our food choices.

"Mooo!"
Bessy The Cow

To many of us, it seems our beef comes only from freezers or restaurants. But before that, it was a cow, and before that, it was the food that cow ate, and the land, water, and energy needed to create that food.

COWS EAT—WHILE HUMANS STARVE

Every day, 40,000 children starve to death.[105] And every day, the United States grows enough grain to provide every human on Earth with two loaves of bread.[106] Where does that food go? It's obviously not all feeding hungry children. Much of it is gobbled up by animals that are destined for our stomachs.

> *"Tonight when you go to sleep, in towns all over the United States, there will be little girls and boys who will go to sleep hungry, wishing for some food to fill their empty stomachs. And as they dream of the food that won't be on the table the next morning, all over the country, livestock will be stuffed to the hilt on the very crops that could be feeding these children."*
>
> Harvey Diamond, *Your Heart, Your Planet*

The Wall Street Journal reports that U.S. livestock eat enough grain and soybeans to feed over five times the number of people in the U.S.[107] How can this be? It is because cows consume a great deal of food. It takes up to 16 pounds of grain and soybeans to produce just one pound of feedlot beef.[108] In the U.S., 80% of the corn and over 95% of the oats grown are fed to livestock, not humans.[109]

"WASTING OUR FOOD?"

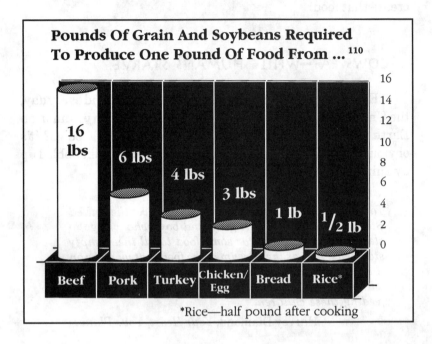

Pounds Of Grain And Soybeans Required To Produce One Pound Of Food From ... [110]

Beef — 16 lbs
Pork — 6 lbs
Turkey — 4 lbs
Chicken/Egg — 3 lbs
Bread — 1 lb
Rice* — 1/2 lb

*Rice—half pound after cooking

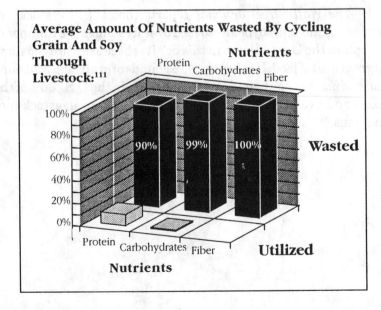

Average Amount Of Nutrients Wasted By Cycling Grain And Soy Through Livestock: [111]

Protein — 90%
Carbohydrates — 99%
Fiber — 100%

Wasted / Utilized

Nutrients

In the U.S. today, 60 million acres of land are being used to grow food for people. This is a land mass about the size of Oregon.[112] Meanwhile, 1.2 billion acres are growing food for livestock. That's an area about the size of Texas, California, Montana, New Mexico, Arizona, Nevada, Colorado, Wyoming, North Dakota, South Dakota, Pennsylvania, New York, North Carolina, South Carolina, Florida, Georgia, Illinois, Wisconsin, Indiana, Kentucky, Tennessee, Virginia, West Virginia, and Maine combined.[113] We're using all that land to produce beef, but we're not getting much out of it.

The University of California estimates that a healthy acre of prime land can grow 40,000 pounds of potatoes, or it can produce 250 pounds of beef.[114] Other studies say that it can take 500 times more land to make a pound of beef than a pound of vegetables.[115] In a world where a child dies of malnutrition every three seconds, this is a tragic way to use our land.

There are now more people going to bed hungry every night than at any time in human history.[116] On this same planet, many of the people who eat a meat-based diet are trying to lose weight. While 40,000 children are dying of starvation every day, 80% of the nine-year-old girls in California have already been on their first diet.[117] There's a connection between these two realities. The production of the meat that is making many Americans fat is using up much of the Earth's agricultural resources, leaving little to feed the world's poor.

If we really want an end to world hunger, we might consider the impact modern meat production has on global food supplies. If Americans reduced their meat consumption by only ten percent for one year, enough grain would be freed up that we could feed everybody who will starve to death this year.[118]

> *"The day that hunger is eradicated from the Earth there will be the greatest spiritual explosion the world has ever known. Humanity cannot imagine the joy that will burst into the world on the day of that great revolution."*
>
> Frederico Garcia Lorca,
> Spanish poet and dramatist

RAUNCHY MOUNTAINS

Unfortunately, the wasted food we give cows doesn't disappear. Like any animal, cows make manure. Farmers used to make fertilizer out of manure—it was a form of recycling. But in modern agriculture, the animals are so densely packed together that the manure is often unmanageable, and it gets piled up into mountains.[119] Every second, U.S. livestock produce 250,000 pounds of excrement—more than enough to fill a typical family's home.[120]

> *"One cow produces as much waste as 16 humans. With 20,000 animals in our pens, we have a problem equal to a city of 320,000 people."*
>
> Harry J. Webb, President
> Blair Cattle Company, Blair, Nebraska

What can a rancher on a limited budget do with all that manure? Much of it is handled carelessly, often ending up in our water. And so do the nitrates and other agricultural chemicals that are used in the production of beef. Carol Close, a resident of Southern California, wonders if her child's birth defects could have anything to do with the nitrates from the manure released into water near her. In the 1991 PBS documentary *Diet for a New America*, she said,

> *"The water quality control board came out and tested our water. And they said that it was contaminated with nitrates. We were really shocked. And then we started wondering about the health effects for our children . . . I wondered if my children had experienced any loss of oxygen that could have hurt their mental development. I worried about problems that might come up in the future. I worried about my neighbors who were still drinking the water, and that they might get cancer. I worried about everybody in our town that never had their water tested. I worried that they would never know."*

WHEN THE WELLS RUN DRY

Modern beef production not only pollutes our water, it wastes it.

Born in the Rocky Mountains, the magnificent Colorado River rushes through Utah, the Grand Canyon, Nevada, and finally Mexico before reaching the Gulf of California. For thousands of years, the Colorado River has provided life-giving water to the regions that surround it. For thousands of years, this river has triumphantly completed its long journey by thrusting its way into the ocean. Today, the Colorado River is disappearing rapidly. At certain times of the year, this fountain of life peters out to no more than a trickle by the time it reaches the sea.

What is destroying the mighty Colorado River? Beef production is a primary culprit.

Beneath the high plains states of Colorado, Kansas, Nebraska, Oklahoma, and New Mexico lies the mighty Ogallala Aquifer. It took nature millions of years to create this glorious pool of pure, fresh water. It has taken humans only a few decades to bring this miracle of nature into danger. More than 13 trillion gallons of water are being taken from the enormous aquifer every year. More water is withdrawn from the Ogallala than is used to grow all the fruits and vegetables in the U.S. Water resource experts estimate that at the current rate of water consumption, the Ogallala Aquifer may be exhausted in 35 years.[121] Why is so much water being drained from this aquifer? Beef production.

The high plains states depend on the Ogallala for their survival. If it runs dry, these states may become uninhabitable for human beings.[122]

Wherever you live, good, clean, drinkable water is precious. In California, where years of drought have frequently left grass brown and trees dying, people will go to great lengths to save water. Some even shower less often or flush the toilet just once a day.

"If it's yellow, let it mellow; if it's brown, flush it down."
common phrase on California bathroom walls

These measures do help to save water, but not much. The reason is that most of the U.S.'s water isn't going to showers and toilets, or even to swimming pools and golf courses. More than half of all the water consumed in the United States—including water from the Colorado River and the Ogallala Aquifer—is being poured on the land growing food for animals and used to wash away their manure.[123]

"The water that goes into a 1,000 pound steer would float a naval destroyer."

Newsweek, *February 22, 1981*

The production of a typical pound of beef in the United States requires 2,500 gallons of water.[124] By comparison, if you take five showers every week, each shower is five minutes long, and your shower has a flow rate of four gallons per minute, you're going to use 2,500 gallons of water about every six months. What would you rather do to save 2,500 gallons of water? Not eat a pound of beef or not shower for six months?

TRADING FORESTS FOR BURGERS?

While many cows live in feedlots where they are fattened up with grain and soybeans, some still graze in fields. Unfortunately, that's often not much better. Overgrazing is so common that it's considered normal. Cows eat the bigger plants, and their hooves trample the smaller ones. When many cows are on one piece of land, it usually ends up as a desert. The next step is to cut down forests to make up for the lost grazing land. And so it goes. Our forests keep on shrinking, and our deserts continue to expand.

In all, 260 million acres of forested U.S. land have been cleared to create land for animal agriculture.[125] That's more than an acre for every U.S. citizen.

If we reduced our meat consumption, much of that land could be replanted with trees.

THAT'S NOT ALL, FOLKS, . . .

The devastating impact of beef production seems to be everywhere—trampling out and chewing up huge amounts of resources. But not many people would have guessed how much beef contributes to global warming and the energy crisis.

Forests are the Earth's storage banks for carbon dioxide (CO_2). When we burn trees to create cattle pasture, we release their stored CO_2 into the atmosphere, polluting our air and adding to global warming. When *U.S. News & World Report* featured our endangered planet Earth on its cover, their report stated:

> *"Grazing land of tropical rainforest needed for ¼ lb. of beef—55 square feet*
> *CO_2 emitted by clearing 55 square feet of tropical rainforest—500 pounds*
> *Some 138 million pounds of beef were imported from Central America last year."*

The report also said that the average automobile in the United States is responsible for putting five tons (10,000 pounds) of CO_2 into the atmosphere each year.[126] That means we can save more CO_2 from entering our atmosphere by not eating five pounds of rainforest beef than by not driving a car for a year. Further, the production, transportation, refrigeration, and packaging of beef (and of all the water and grain that go into it) use up additional amounts of energy, contributing to global warming, air pollution, and acid rain.

> *"Few of us, indeed, understand what scope of energy is required to supply us with our meat-based diet. To describe it as colossal would be a gross understatement."*
> Harvey Diamond, *Your Heart, Your Planet*

Seventeen percent of the U.S.'s energy use is for food production.[127] Experts conclude that a meat-based diet is responsible for using up at least 20 times more energy than a vegetarian diet.[128]

While beef production takes a greater environmental toll than any other meat, all of the mass-produced animal products we consume in North America use up enormous amounts of resources and cause a great deal of pollution. By choosing not to eat industrialized meat, we take a powerful stand for the future of life on Earth.

> *"A reduction in meat consumption is the most potent single act you can take to halt the destruction of our environment and preserve our precious natural resources."*
> John Robbins, *Our Food, Our World*

GOOD FOR OUR PLANET, AND GOOD FOR YOU TOO

At age 65, Joe Smith died in the intensive care unit of his local hospital. After his death, a doctor opened up his chest. The doctor found the artery that had become clogged, cut it open, and pulled out the waxy, fatty material that had caked against the walls of Joe's coronary artery, blocking the flow of blood to his heart and killing him.

What was that fatty material that caused the death of Joe Smith? It was the result of years of eating foods high in saturated fat and cholesterol.

Joe Smith died of heart disease. If the vein that had become clogged had led to Joe's brain, he would have had a stroke. Millions of people share these diseases. As North Americans, we have a greater than 50% chance of dying from a disease caused by our arteries becoming clogged.[129] We would have better odds flipping a coin. But if we cut our meat consumption in half, our chances of dying from heart disease would drop to 30%.[130] If we were to eliminate meat from our diet, we would cut our risk of heart disease down to 15%.[131]

Even so, some people are afraid and ask, "Are vegetarians as healthy as meat-eaters?" According to scientific research, they're not. They're healthier.

"Vegetarians have the best diet. They . . . have a fraction of our heart attack rate and they have only 40 percent of our cancer rate. They outlive us. On the average they outlive other men (and women) by about six years now."

William Castelli, M.D., Director
The Framingham Heart Study

Can we get enough protein without eating meat? Totally. The food and nutrition board of the USDA says humans should get 6% of their daily calories from protein. With that in mind, take a look at the chart below.

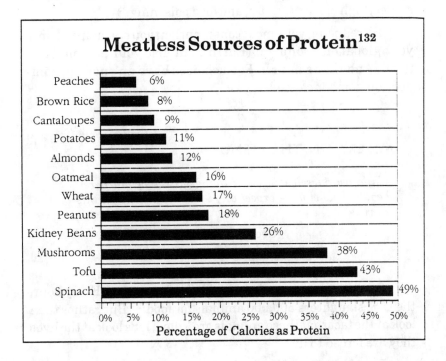

Meatless Sources of Protein[132]

Food	Percentage of Calories as Protein
Peaches	6%
Brown Rice	8%
Cantaloupes	9%
Potatoes	11%
Almonds	12%
Oatmeal	16%
Wheat	17%
Peanuts	18%
Kidney Beans	26%
Mushrooms	38%
Tofu	43%
Spinach	49%

Some people think meat is a better source for protein than these vegetarian foods. But it just isn't so.

> *"Formerly, vegetable proteins were classified as second-class, and regarded as inferior to first-class proteins of animal origin, but this distinction has now been generally discarded."*
>
> Lancet, a medical journal

High levels of meat consumption contribute to many diseases. These include cancers of the breast, prostate, and colon, as well as osteoporosis, arthritis, asthma, multiple sclerosis, diabetes, hypoglycemia, ulcers, constipation, obesity, kidney stones, gallstones, high blood pressure, and food poisoning.[133]

By reducing your meat consumption, you can help not only your global environment (Earth), but also your personal one (you). And that's not all. Food choices have an enormous impact on someone else . . . .

MISERY ON THE MENU

> *"While we ourselves are the living graves of murdered beasts, how can we expect any ideal conditions on this Earth?"*
>
> George Bernard Shaw,
> playwright and philosopher

Of course, meat requires the death of an animal. Every hour, the U.S. slaughters 500,000 animals for food.[134] But rather than look at the fact that these animals are killed, let's look at the lives they are forced to live.

Ronald McDonald tells children that "hamburgers grow in hamburger patches and love to be eaten." But the truth is that most modern meat is raised in "factory farms."[135] Here, the farmers cram their cows, pigs, and chickens into steel cages sometimes several animals per cage.[136] The animals often stand in

Meat Consumption, Heart Disease, and Bowel Cancer— A Remarkable Parallel*

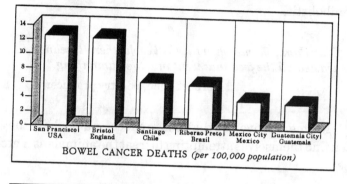

BOWEL CANCER DEATHS *(per 100,000 population)*

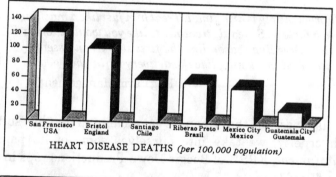

HEART DISEASE DEATHS *(per 100,000 population)*

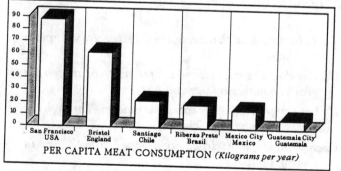

PER CAPITA MEAT CONSUMPTION *(Kilograms per year)*

*Data from *Journal of the National Cancer Institute,* Vol. 51, No. 6, Dec. 1973; and *Foreign Agricultural Circular - Livestock and Meat,* USDA, Washington, D.C., 1976

their own excrement or drop it on the heads of those below.[137] Many will never see the light of the sun or have a breath of fresh air. These conditions are so unnatural to the modern cow, pig, or chicken, that the animals are sometimes driven completely insane. Chickens, for example, often attack each other—even becoming cannibalistic.

"It's a damn shame when they kill each other. It means we wasted all the feed that went into the damn thing."
Herbert Reed, poultry producer

Farmers, driven by the need to cut costs anywhere they can, often find themselves attempting to treat the animals as merchandise.

"Forget the pig is an animal. Treat him just like a machine in a factory. Schedule treatments like you would lubrication. Breeding season like the first step in an assembly line. And marketing like the delivery of finished goods."
Hog Farm Management

Is it possible that when we eat an animal that has suffered such cruelty, we take into ourselves some of its pain? In *Edutainment*, KRS-1 of Boogie Down Productions raps in their song, "Beef,"

"Let us begin now with the cow, the way it gets to your plate and how.
The cow doesn't grow fast enough for man, so through his greed he makes a faster plan.
He has drugs to make the cow grow quicker. Through the stress the cow gets sicker.
Twenty-one different drugs are pumped, into the cow in one big lump.
So just before it dies, it cries, in the slaughterhouse full of germs and flies.
Off with their head, they pack it, drain it, and cart it, and there it is—in your local supermarket.

Fresh and bloody, a corpse neatly packed. And you wonder about heart attacks?

Come on now man, let's be for real, you are what you eat—is the way I feel . . .

"In your body its structure becomes your structure—all the fear and stress of another.

Fear and stress can become a part of you, in your cells and blood, this is true . . .

Life brings life. Death brings death. Keep on eating the dead, and what's left? . . .

How many cows must be pumped up fatter?

How many rats gotta fall in the batter? . . .

If you'll consume, the FDA could care less.

They'll sell you donkey meat and say it's fresh!"

In our food choices, we have power. We have the power to support—or not support—the exploitation and killing of billions of animals. We have the power to be a part of the environmental problems—or their solutions. And we have the power to take responsibility for our own health. Every single meal counts.

(For more information and support, we strongly suggest you join EarthSave, 706 Frederick St., Santa Cruz, CA 95062 (408) 423-4069. EarthSave works to educate people on how their food choices affect their health, happiness, and the future of life on Earth.)

FOOD CHOICES FOR OUR FUTURE

◆ Eat less industrialized meat, or none.

◆ Eat more pastas, potatoes, soups, vegetable stews, bread, burritos, sandwiches, stir fries, tofu burgers, pizzas, salads, rice, beans, casseroles, steamed vegetables, fruit, and cereals.

+ Donate time or food to a local food bank. To locate the food bank nearest you, call or write Second Harvest, 116 South Michigan Avenue, Suite 4, Chicago, IL 60603 (312) 263-2303.

+ Get school(s) to offer a vegetarian lunch option. Do you think school lunches could maybe, just possibly, improve a little bit? A majority of students would like their school to offer a meat-free choice if it doesn't already. If you want help, contact EarthSave. They have a "Healthy People, Healthy Planet" school lunch program and can give you resources and support in this endeavor.

+ Read *Diet for a New America* if you want to learn more about how our food choices affect our world. It's also a good source of information for people who want to learn about the environmental and health effects of eating pigs, chickens, and fish (as well as beef). Give it to friends if you want to educate them. You can also watch the award-winning PBS documentary *Diet for a New America* and show it to friends or to classes in school(s). The book can be ordered for $17.95 (including postage and handling) from EarthSave. The video can also be ordered from EarthSave—for $23.95 (including postage and handling). To order either of these great resources, call (800)-362-3648.

Chapter Seven

EATING FOR A HEALTHY WORLD

Environmentally conscious food choices go beyond whether or not we eat animals. Everything on our plate effects our health and our world.

POISONING OUR FOOD AND OUR FARMERS

Farmers use pesticides to kill bugs that eat their crops. Every year, farmers pour 1.5 billion pounds of pesticides onto American farmlands.[138] Many of these poisons were originally developed during World War II to kill people.

In 1900, one out of every 33 Americans died of cancer. Today, one out of every three Americans dies of cancer.[139] Why has there been such a huge increase? Exposure to modern pesticides, which didn't exist in 1900, is thought to be one of the primary reasons.[140] Dozens of the poisons sprayed on food crops are known to cause cancer.[141] Pesticide exposure is also linked to hypertension, Parkinson's disease, epilepsy, cardiovascular disorders, birth defects, and many other major health problems.[142] Let's face it: Pouring poisons on our food is a dangerous thing to do.

Not all of the pesticides sprayed on food will stay there. Much of them wash off, ending up in our water. Pesticides used in California's San Joaquin Valley, the nation's richest agricultural region, have seeped into underground reservoirs over a 7,000 square mile area, contaminating the drinking water of a million residents.[143]

"The problem with my child was caused by the chemicals in the fields and in the water. This is what my doctor told me. We stay not because we want to, but because these problems make it so nobody wants to buy our house."

Nora Gonzalez, McFarland, Calif.

Some people have started to fight back against the poisons that are causing them such hardships. In 1993, the California town of Sanger won a $15 million suit against Dow Chemical Company and several other companies that had poisoned their water with DBCP, a pesticide used to kill worms that causes cancer and damages the reproductive organs in humans.[144] These people fought back because they knew their water had been poisoned. But many people who have polluted water don't know it.

Pesticides have been detected in the ground water of 23 states as a result of agriculture.[145] The use of these poisons doesn't just affect consumers and our water supply. Consider the farm workers . . . .

"Always we notice the powder of the pesticides on the leaves. I was working in the fields from the beginning of my pregnancy. I was groggy from the Cesarean when the doctor told me, 'I have bad news.' He simply said Felipe was born without arms or legs. His father was crying. And my mother even more. When we first saw him, we felt a great sadness. The doctors told me it was because of the pesticides."

Ramona Franco, grape picker, Delano, Calif.

In the U.S., well over seven million people work with pesticides on the job.[146] Growing food with pesticides is so commonplace that it's considered normal. As long as we choose to buy food grown with pesticides, farmers will continue to use them, we will continue to eat poisonous residues, and the farm workers will suffer.

Sometimes, pesticides are sprayed on more than fields. In 1990, many southern Californians were angered by the sound of helicopters spraying malathion (a dangerous pesticide) across much of the city. Malathion was sprayed because a crop-eating variety of fruit fly pests had been discovered in Los Angeles. People were told that the pesticide was completely safe, but they were also told to keep their pets and children indoors and to cover their cars. The mist of poison was sprayed from the sky, coating large portions of the city, eating the paint off cars and causing sickness in hundreds of residents. The result of this project? Unsuccessful. The crop-eating fruit flies continue to haunt California's agriculture.

Do we need pesticides to kill bugs? No. Farmers spend one billion dollars every year on agricultural chemicals. Yet in 1989, the National Academy of Sciences reported that farmers who apply little or no pesticides to crops produce as much bug-free food as those who use large quantities of them.[147]

Why does anybody use pesticides? Because farming without them usually requires more personpower and fewer machines. That means it's going to create more jobs, but it might also cost more money.

Researchers and farmers have spent decades developing the most productive methods for farming with pesticides. But there hasn't been as much research on how to grow food more organically, so that method might cost more for a time, until we discover new techniques. Nevertheless, a wealth of wisdom in the area of non-toxic agriculture already exists. For example, farmers can use lady bugs, whose favorite food is the bugs that destroy crops, as a natural pesticide. Farmers can also rotate and mix crops, and they can use compost to create healthier soil and more bug-resistant plants. Since many "conventional" farmers don't know much about natural pest-control, training will also be needed.

Organic farming doesn't just prevent pesticides from being used. It's also more energy efficient, resource conserving, environmentally sound, health-giving, sustainable, and productive.

THE CHOICE TO BUY ORGANIC

Farmers grow what people want to buy. If we buy more organic food, we will make growing it profitable and help our agricultural system to shift away from poisons and towards a healthier system of food production.

Organic food is often more costly to the consumer than its "conventional" counterparts. But the more organic food we buy, the cheaper it will become. Every time we buy organic food, we contribute to our own health, the health of the farm workers, and the employment of more people and fewer machines.

You can visit your local natural foods stores and see which one has the best supply of organic foods.

(Call or write for a free copy of
Organic Food Mail Order Supplies; see page 161.)

LONG DISTANCE FOOD

"Last year, New York area residents bought 24,000 tons of broccoli—importing almost all of it from the West Coast, nearly 2,700 miles away. The cost: $6 million for transportation alone. What's more, refrigerated broccoli loses 19 percent of its vitamin C in 24 hours, 34 percent in two days.

The absurdity is this: Broccoli prefers cool weather and could have been grown at home, providing additional jobs and income to New York residents . . . Last year, New Yorkers spent $1 billion on food transportation . . . For every two dollars we spend to grow food, we spend another dollar to move it around. Not just to New York. Massachusetts imports more than 80 percent of its food, and

Pennsylvania—a leading agricultural state in the U.S.—more than 70 percent."

> excerpted from *The Tarrytown Letter*
> September, 1984

Most food goes through quite a journey in getting from the farm to our shopping carts. First, it is grown and harvested, and then it must be trucked to a collection center. Next, the food travels hundreds or even thousands of miles to a distribution center, then is trucked to stores, and finally put out on the shelves where we can buy it. The typical mouthful of American food travels 1,300 miles from the farm to the dinner plate.[148] All this transportation uses up energy and releases huge amounts of carbon dioxide into our atmosphere. Food that has been through all this may also be weeks old.

THE CHOICE FOR FARMERS' MARKETS

"Tired of long, quiet, narrow supermarket aisles; of produce packaged in plastic, frozen into little briquettes or caked with wax? Depressed by the sight of those sad, tired, droopy heads of lettuce; rock-hard, anemic-looking tomatoes or apples that glare back at you under the hum of fluorescent lights? If you are, then farmers' markets are definitely what you're looking for."

> Jeffrey Hollender,
> *How To Make The World A Better Place*

Thousands of farmers' markets have opened across the U.S. Dozens of farmers come to these markets to sell produce directly to people, without the distributors and stores that would otherwise come between the grower and the consumer.[149] The food is usually fresh, organic, and often cheaper than from supermarkets.

JOINING A LOCAL FOOD CO-OP

There are more than 4,000 food co-ops and buying clubs in the United States. Eighty percent of them carry organic produce. Compared to supermarkets or natural foods stores, their prices are likely to be 5%-30% less, and their selection is probably larger.[150] Co-ops often use the volunteer labor of their members, so you might have to pitch in and help for a few hours a month. If you live in a rural community and don't have access to big stores nearby, co-ops are probably the best way to have fresh and organic food.

(For the name and address of your closest co-op,
see page 161.)

GROW A GREAT GARDEN!

It can be easy for us to lose connection with one of the primary sustaining forces in our lives: food. Gardening is one way to learn about and enjoy fresh, free, and delicious organic food and to come back into contact with Earth. It can also be an enjoyable, nourishing experience.

In our society, far more space is given over to lawns than to gardens. If everyone in North America converted their lawns to vegetable gardens, we would be able to grow all of our own food.[151] Our lawns could become the bread-baskets of the continent. If you grow food for yourself, you can also be sure that it's organic.

Home gardens usually grow food that tastes better, and because of the personal care they receive, home gardens produce an average of five times more food per square foot than commercial agriculture.[152] Many of us want to eat more locally grown food. How much more local can you get than your own backyard?

(For information on organic gardening and how to do it,
contact Rodale Press; see page 161.)

START OR JOIN A COMMUNITY GARDEN

Whether you live in the city or in the country, community gardening is an enjoyable and effective way to provide food while building a community and empowering yourself and others. You can start almost anywhere: on the grounds of a church, in the back of a school, in your own or a friend's backyard, on an abandoned lot, on a roof-top, or on land contributed by local officials.

Some community gardens are divided up, with each person or family having their own area. Others work cooperatively, often dividing up the food or donating it to needy families, food banks, or soup kitchens. And there are some community gardeners who sell their food.

WHAT'S FOR DINNER?

Many corporations would like nothing better than for our generation to live our whole lives as predictable consumers of their products. Many of them want us to remain addicted to what they sell, even if it is killing us and our world. And yet because of the dangers facing the future, our society must move away from its addiction to meat, over-processed foods, and destructive growing methods if we are to survive.

Many of us buy food habitually, not consciously. As we learn more about how our food choices affect our world, we have the opportunity to re-evaluate them.

"Loyalty to a petrified opinion never yet broke a chain or freed a human soul."

Mark Twain

Each of us can make our food choices into a statement of our values. We can use buying food, growing gardens, and eating as an opportunity to take a powerful stand for what we believe.

If we want to . . . .

The choice is ours.

Chapter Eight

ENERGY CHOICES

Energy is the force that gives us zest for life. It's what makes our bodies move, our minds function, and our hearts sing. Energy is power, joy, and enthusiasm. It can enable us to run marathons, to passionately express ourselves, and even to survive high school. Without energy, we can become bored, wilted, and lifeless couch potatoes.

Energy flows through every human, television, tree, electric guitar, animal, car, star, and light bulb. Energy is the essence of all life. Plants get their energy from the sun. Toasters get their energy by plugging into an electrical current.

THE POWER OF THE SWITCH

Many of us can flip on a switch or turn a key and instantly have heat, light, transportation, or entertainment. Our energy comes to us so easily that many of us rarely think about its origins. As a result, we can easily forget energy has any history at all. But in reality, there is a long and often deadly chain of events that leads to our power outlets and gas tanks.

Where do our light bulbs, automobiles, and refrigerators get most of their power from? The burning of the Earth's fossil fuels, specifically oil, coal, and natural gas.[153]

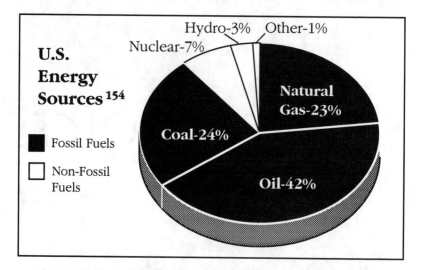

U.S. Energy Sources [154]

■ Fossil Fuels

□ Non-Fossil Fuels

Hydro-3% Other-1%
Nuclear-7%
Natural Gas-23%
Coal-24%
Oil-42%

The supply of fossil fuels is far from unlimited. The U.S. already imports almost half of the fossil fuels it burns.[155] At current rates of consumption, by 2020 the domestic supply of fossil fuels may run dry. By 2040, the entire world is expected to run out.[156]

While fossil fuels give many wonderful things to modern society, they also charge our world an enormous price. Every time we turn on a light switch or start a car, we may be adding our signature to the lethal smoke that is polluting our air, water, and land.

THE RAIN THAT BURNS

Rain cleanses and refreshes the air. It waters Earth's vegetation and fills rivers and lakes with a fresh supply of water. One good rain can turn vast African deserts into glorious meadows filled with blooming flowers and vibrant life. All the plants, trees, and creatures in the world depend on this precious liquid for their survival. If you've ever been in a smoggy city, you may have noticed how rain washes pollution out of the air. Even cities with the most polluted air can enjoy clear blue skies after a good rain.

But today, in many parts of the world, rain has become a source of danger. The falling rain picks up sulfur dioxides, nitrogen oxides, carbon dioxide, and some of the other pollutants emitted in the burning of fossil fuels. This can cause the rain to become more acidic than vinegar, leading to the term "acid rain." There is also "acid snow," "acid fog," and "acid hail."

Thousands of people from all over the world once climbed Fichtelburg Mountain in Europe to marvel at the awesome view from its mighty peaks. Looking out from this mountaintop, they could see extraordinary expanses of pristine ancient forest. But now, when people arrive at the summit and look out at the view, they see dead trees and barren brown patches where forests once stood.[157] These woods have fallen victim to acid rain, as have 35% of Europe's forests.[158]

Acid rain is hitting North America hard too. It's led to the death of so many maple trees in New England and eastern Canada that their maple syrup industries may end by the turn of the century.[159] Acid rain is destroying trees and lakes, eroding buildings, and killing animals and people.

Once acidified rain has reached Earth, it often joins our drinking water. As it travels through our drinking water pipes, it may leach out lead, cadmium, aluminum, and asbestos.[160] These materials are poisonous and can lead to kidney damage, Parkinson's disease, brain damage, respiratory problems, Alzheimer's disease, and increased risk of heart problems.[161] A congressional study cited acid rain as a factor leading to 50,000 premature deaths ever year.[162] Every time we turn on a power switch or start up a car, we may be contributing to rain that burns. We also add to another problem you've probably heard a great deal about . . . .

GLOBAL WARMING

"Very soon, the Earth will become hotter than at any time in human history. As the continents warm and the ice at the poles melts, oceans will rise, droughts will devastate

crops, and entire species of plants and animals will
become extinct. It now seems evident that this extremely
rapid warming is being caused by us, the humans."
  Albert K. Bates, *Climate In Crisis*

To get a sense of how global warming works, imagine a car with all the windows rolled up on a hot day. What happens? The heat from the sun gets trapped inside the car by all the glass. The car gets hot! The same thing happens on a global scale.

When we burn fossil fuels for energy, carbon dioxide and other gases are released, surrounding our planet like a blanket. Just like glass, these gases capture the heat. For millenniums, there's been a fairly stable level of carbon dioxide in our atmosphere, enabling Earth's average temperature to remain consistent.[163]

In the last century, carbon dioxide levels in our atmosphere have increased by more than 25%.[164] The six hottest years in recorded history have all occurred since 1980.[165] This has made portions of polar ice caps melt on both ends of the Earth, causing the oceans to rise by four to eight inches in the last century.[166] And global warming has only barely begun. Scientists predict that in 50 years the Earth will be three to five degrees hotter than it is today.[167] This would lead to the melting of far larger chunks of the polar ice caps and a rise of up to 14 feet in global sea levels.[168]

With a substantial rise in sea levels, we would see massive floods. Changing weather patterns could lead to droughts in some places and torrential rain in others.[169] It could become difficult to grow food on planet Earth.[170] Billions of people could starve to death. Some scientists also fear global warming could cause so much water to evaporate that the Earth would be surrounded in clouds, bringing on the next ice age. So far, climate destabilization has mainly been noticed by scientists and environmentalists. But in the years to come, it may have a substantial impact on all of us. Only time will tell if we will make wise choices or continue to create global warming and a possible ice age.

Our climate is being altered, our air is being polluted, and our rain is becoming a hazard. The driving forces behind each of these problems are the enormous quantities of fossil fuels our society burns for energy. We are using this energy as electricity, heat, and power for machines and automobiles.

OOPS!

To use oil for fuel, we often need to ship it across great distances. But some of it never reaches its destination; ships sometimes spill their cargo. Every year, our fossil fuel industry dumps more than 3 million metric tons of oil into the sea.[171] You may remember the Valdez oil spill in Alaska. Much of the world saw pictures of blackened sea lions and dying birds. Once the media hype of that spill began to fizzle away, so did people's awareness of oil spills. But the spills go on, and marine life continues to die. Even a relatively small oil spill, like the one that occurred in the Wadden Sea in 1969, can kill more than 40,000 seabirds.[172]

It can be easy to blame oil spills on one person or one company. When the Valdez spill happened, many people blamed it on the drunk Captain Hazelwood of the Exxon ship. But as Greenpeace put it, "It wasn't his driving that caused the Alaskan oil spill. It was yours." Every time we drive, we contribute to oil spills around the world.

THE TRANSFORMATION OF TRANSPORTATION

Before there were cars, people walked, jogged, and rode bikes or horses, getting exercise and experiencing the natural environment around them. But today, when we travel in cars, we get into a machine that seals us off from the elements of nature. The rain could be pouring down, yet we would be dry. The air might be cold, but we would stay warm. Our cars insulate us, keeping us from coming into contact with nature.

Inside a car, we can travel at 60 miles an hour while our bodies sit almost motionless. Advertising tells us that cars are sexy, glamorous, and expressions of power. But actually they enable us to travel great distances under conditions of boring monotony. People traveling through a forest might have once savored the sweet smells and beautiful views, but today we travel with our attention mostly focused on cement and road signs. And everywhere we go in these massive machines, we guzzle gasoline and spew out pollution.

Most vehicles are like small power plants on wheels, using gasoline as their source of fuel. Their tail pipes are like mini-smokestacks, spilling out poisons. Driving causes more atmospheric pollution than any other human activity. Every year, the average American car adds to global warming and acid rain by emitting five tons of carbon dioxide.[173] Our cars also produce many other toxic and even poisonous gases that pollute the air we breathe.

DRIVING US CRAZY

You probably have known that the world's human population is increasing dangerously. So is the world's car population. In 1970, there were 200 million cars in the world. In 1990, there were almost 500 million.[174]

It's rush hour on a freeway in a big city. The air is hot and reeks with the smell of exhaust from the cars ahead. It's taken half an hour to drive the last mile, and we know that the worst is yet to come, because it's only five in the afternoon. All around, horns are honking. The tension of exhausted and frustrated drivers fills the air so intensely that people have been known to kill strangers with guns.

As the world's vehicle populations go up, traffic congestion can only get worse. Although the average speed in Los Angeles was 33 mph in 1990, experts predict that because of increasing traffic, the year 2000 will see L.A.'s average speed drop to 15 mph.[175] Scientists forecast that if car populations continue to rise for another 30 years, traffic congestion will become ten times worse than it is today.[176] This means more pollution as idling vehicles burn gasoline without going anywhere. Driving delays are expected to contribute 73 million tons of carbon dioxide to global warming over the next two decades.[177]

We're back on a congested road at rush hour. But this time we're in the car-pool lane, comfortably cruising at 55 mph past three bumper-to-bumper lanes that look like parking lots. Looking at the heads of the people in the cars we're passing, we notice all the vacant seats.

What would it be like if each car contained more than one person? For one thing, the number of cars on the road would be cut in half. For another thing,

"*If each commuter car carried just one more person (for a day), we'd save 600 thousand gallons of gasoline ... and would prevent 12 million pounds of carbon dioxide from polluting the atmosphere.*"

The Earth Works Group
50 Simple Things You Can Do To Save The Earth

Car-pooling is an important improvement, but it's not the whole solution. If we want a healthy future, we'll need to take a good look at our driving habits and consider the alternatives.

FINDING A BETTER WAY

Do you care about our future? Most of us do. Actions, however, speak even louder than words.

Do you have a bike? If so, how often do you ride it? Bikes are a wonderful and inexpensive way to get exercise, save energy, enjoy the world around us, and journey from one place to another. The bicycle is one of the most efficient uses of human muscle power. In many parts of the world, bicycles are the main form of transportation. In China, there are 540 of them for every car.[178] And they're making a comeback in North America too. U.S. bicycle transportation has tripled since 1977.[179]

Do you ever ride on public transportation? Even though buses emit large amounts of pollution, they are still far less polluting than personal vehicles. Trains and subways are better still. By riding on mass transit, you also cut down on traffic congestion and support an industry that becomes stronger with every person who uses it.

Do you have a car? If so, how often do you drive it? The average American car burns almost one and a half gallons of gasoline every day.[180] By driving less, we can not only save gasoline, we can also save carbon dioxide and many other gases from being emitted into our atmosphere.

If you drive, do you drive fast? Did you know that driving 75 mph uses up 20% more gasoline than driving 55 mph to go the same distance and that driving faster can also lead to more accidents?[181] Sometimes, when irresponsible drivers speed to get somewhere faster, they never get there at all. Car accidents kill 47,000 people every year in the U.S.—the same number of Americans as died in the entire Vietnam war.[182] Many more are seriously injured.

If you have a car, do you know how many miles it runs for every gallon of gas it burns?

Check this out: In the 12 months before Iraq's 1990 invasion of Kuwait, the U.S. imported 292 million barrels of oil from Iraq and Kuwait combined.[183] An improvement of three miles per gallon (mpg) in our domestic motor vehicles would save that much annually. An improvement of seven mpg would save as much oil as we imported from the entire Persian Gulf region in 1990.[184] The average American new car made in 1994 got 26 mpg. Some cars got as little as eight mpg, others as much as 56 mpg. If you have a car, where does it fit into this spectrum? When we buy the more fuel-efficient models, we save money and gasoline, and we also encourage car companies to come out with even more efficient cars in the years ahead.

FUEL EFFICIENCY FOR THE FUTURE

There are many new forms of transportation that are not yet commercially available in the U.S., but that probably will be changing soon. Each of these is a source of hope and possibility; they can play a part in lowering the amount of fossil fuels we use and in making our world a safer place.

Consider, for example, the Volvo LCP 2000. This vehicle gets an average of 73 miles to the gallon. You might think that a car with that kind of mileage would lack zip. But this car can accelerate faster than the average car and has a top speed of well over 100 mph.[185]

An Audi 100 luxury sedan was adapted for fuel economy and then traveled 3,000 miles through Europe without re-fueling, averaging 133 miles per gallon. Citröen, GM, Honda, Nissan, Volkswagen, and others have developed low-pollution prototype cars that get between 68 and 130 mpg.[186]

A North American fleet of cars getting the kind of mileage of even the Volvo LCP 2000 would save 4,500 pounds of global warming-causing carbon dioxide for every person on the continent every year, not to mention huge amounts of carbon monoxide (a lethal poison), radioactive hydrocarbons (which form smog), and nitrogen oxides (which cause acid rain).[187] This step would also save in four months the amount of oil we imported from the entire Persian Gulf in 1986.[188]

POSITIVE ALTERNATIVES

Electric cars are powered by batteries charged from electricity, which can come from the usual sources or from the sun, the wind, biomass, and other non-polluting origins. In the early 1990s, the state of California mandated that by 1998, 2% of the new vehicles sold in the state (about 40,000) should be electric.[189] In response to this announcement, many car companies have created and begun to release electric vehicles that will meet the needs of the times.

Hydrogen, however, may eventually be the best choice for our vehicles. When this gas is combined with oxygen, an explosion occurs that creates water. This explosion can be used to power vehicles. Hydrogen is already being used to fuel buses in Germany, cars in Japan, jet planes in Russia, and American spaceships.[190]

There is an enormous difference between the stuff that leaves the tail pipes of gasoline-powered and hydrogen-powered vehicles. While the vehicle running on gasoline emits pollution, the vehicle running on hydrogen emits clean water.[191] There have been photos taken of engineers lying on their backs behind hydrogen-powered buses, drinking the water that comes out of the bus's exhaust pipes.

We can make hydrogen from sea water. While it takes power to produce hydrogen, this energy can easily come from the sun. Conversion to a hydrogen-based economy could ultimately be less costly than our current fossil-fuel based system.[192]

"The question may not be whether we can afford the transition to a solar-hydrogen energy base, but whether we can afford not to make that switch."
Jay Stein, *The Amicus Journal*, Spring, 1990

PLUGGING THE LEAKS

Imagine an unplugged bathtub being filled with water. To fill the tub, we would need to keep the water pressure extremely high, and the moment we turned off the faucet, the tub would begin to empty. But if we were to plug the hole, we could turn down the faucet and the tub would fill more quickly, remaining filled. Building more power plants is like applying higher water pressure to a leaky tub. Conserving our energy is like plugging the drain. More than ever before, we need to conserve our energy and plug our leaks. Fortunately, the leaks aren't hard to find, and neither are the solutions.

The best way to conserve energy is to start in our own households. New, compact fluorescent light bulbs are one of the first steps we can all take. They produce better quality light with less glare and without the buzz associated with the old fluorescent lights. A single 18 watt, compact fluorescent bulb produces as much light as a typical 75 watt (incandescent) bulb.

Yet over the course of its life, the fluorescent bulb (compared to the incandescent bulb) will save the burning of 770 pounds of coal or 62 gallons of oil—enough to fuel a car from Chicago to Miami.[193]

The cost of this blessing? Nothing. In fact, less than nothing. This one bulb will save up to $100 in electricity costs.[194] Even a 27 watt, compact fluorescent bulb can lead to substantial savings. Compact fluorescent bulbs can seem intimidating, because they are much more costly to begin with. But in the long run, they will save a great deal of money, because they last so much longer and use so much less electricity. Although there are many different types of light bulbs and prices are constantly changing, this chart can give you an idea of how the prices compare.

Comparison Pricing

	Compact Fluorescent	Incandescent
Store price of bulb	$18	$1
Watts used	27	100
Annual energy cost	$5.91	$21.90
Bulbs replaced in 4.5 years	0	10
Total cost after 4.5 years	$44.59	$103.05

In YES!'s home town, the Environmental Council of Santa Cruz helped the local schools retrofit their lighting for improved energy efficiency. The cost of changing the entire district's lights was $380,000, all of which was paid for through a loan. Annual savings today are $160,000, of which $85,000 is going to loan repayment and $75,000 is going to immediate savings for a financially distraught school district. After eight years, the loan will be repaid, and the full $160,000/year will go to the schools. These financial savings represent energy savings equivalent to taking 1,200 cars off the road. The new lights are of higher quality, with less flicker, creating a better classroom environment and less headaches for students. The retrofitting was performed by one of a growing number of environmentally friendly businesses whose work makes the world better.

Why hasn't every school made similar switches already? Because old habits can die hard, and many school administrations are too bureaucratic and too busy to take the time to consider a new idea. That's why YES! started the Green Schools Program, which helps students and teachers make their schools more energy-efficient and environmentally friendly, while saving money at the same time. To get involved, contact YES!.

MORE LEAKS TO PLUG

Inside our homes, we rarely know what the temperature is outside. We keep our homes at "room temperature" by chilling the air if it's hot and heating the air if it's cold. With the simple flip of a switch, we can change the climate of our homes.

We have sweat glands for a reason: they produce moisture that evaporates from our skin to cool us off on hot days. If it's hot out, we can let ourselves know it and be more connected to our local climate by sweating. If we want to be more cool, we can dunk our heads in cold water, dress lightly, or even (in extreme conditions) wear damp clothes. We can also drink cold liquids that will cool us off from the inside. If we plant trees in the proper locations, they can provide shade to our homes, cutting the energy we use for air conditioning in half.[195] These things might seem like common sense, but unfortunately, most Americans aren't practicing them. Isn't it ironic that we are creating global warming by cooling off our air with fossil fuels that make it hotter?

Sixty-four percent of all American homes now have air conditioning.[196] Air conditioners usually use CFCs or other chemicals that destroy our ozone layer and require large amounts of power. If those of us using air conditioners were willing to turn our thermostats up by 4°F, we could save 130,000 barrels of oil daily.[197] If enough of us were willing to use less air conditioning, finding other ways to cool off, the positive impact on our planet would be immeasurable.

Heating our indoor air leads to the emission of more than a billion tons of carbon dioxide into our atmosphere every year.[198] If every U.S. household lowered its average heating temperature by 6°F for a day, we'd save 500,000 barrels of oil.[199] If we were to put on another sweater instead of cranking up the heater, the benefits would be cleaner air and a healthier future for all of us.

There are other things we can do to conserve energy:

+ We can turn down the temperature on our water heater and make sure our hot water tanks are wrapped with insulation.

(Excellent, energy-saving, "on demand" water heaters are available from Real Goods Trading Corporation; see page 162.)

+ We can buy and use more efficient refrigerators and freezers. These appliances use 7% of our nation's electricity. If ever you or your family get a new one, check out the energy-saving models. There are refrigerators and freezers that use only 10% of the energy of conventional models and provide better service.[200] (For information on the most energy-saving models, contact Real Goods.)

+ Huge amounts of warm or cold air are now escaping through our windows. By installing double- or even triple-paned glass, we can cut this energy loss down immensely. If a new brand of "Super Window" that uses special coatings and gases were installed in every American home and office, we would save more than twice as much energy as we now get from Alaska.[201]

As we become more efficient with our life-style, and as our government comes to support efficiency, we will save huge amounts of energy. And we will also save a great deal of money.

"If Americans were now as efficient as our Japanese and Western European competitors are—and even they have a long way to go—we'd save an additional $200 billion a year, which is more than last year's federal budget deficit. Buying the economically optimal amount of energy efficiency for the rest of this century could lead to net savings of several trillion dollars—enough, in principle, to pay off the entire national debt."

Amory Lovins
The Atlantic, December, 1987

CHAPTER NINE

ENERGY AND THE FUTURE OF LIFE

Every morning at the break of dawn, a new day begins. Basking in the sun's warmth and light, plants grow, birds sing, flowers open wide, and people awaken. The abundant energy that streams from the sun gives power to every living thing we know and has been since life on Earth began. Today we can use this precious gift of warmth and light to power our society.

Solar energy, which turns the sun's light into electricity, is the most abundant renewable energy resource.[202] Although it has been more costly than seemingly inexpensive fossil fuels, this is changing. The price of solar electricity dropped 75% in the 1980s and is expected to be financially competitive by the turn of the century.[203] In California, solar electricity can be produced for about eight cents per kilowatt-hour, close to the cost of generating power from fossil fuels in the state.[204]

Luz International of Los Angeles has installed enough solar systems to power 170,000 homes,[205] and 1.2 million homes in the U.S. use solar hot water systems.[206] But we have barely begun to tap the potential of solar power.

There are also other forms of renewable energy. One of them is wind power. California has 15,000 wind mills that produce $200 million worth of electricity every year—enough to power all the homes in San Francisco.[207] Wind power could provide many countries with one-fifth or more of their electricity.[208]

We can also generate energy from biomass, which can be fermented or burned to create fuel or electricity.

"Energy crops of super-fast-growing trees, grasses or shrubs could provide a third or more of the world's supply of electricity and car fuel within thirty years."

Charles Petit, Science Writer
The San Francisco Chronicle, February 11, 1992

When we burn plant materials for energy, we release carbon dioxide, but as the plants grow, they absorb carbon dioxide. This creates a continuous cycle. So with biomass energy, unlike fossil fuels, there is no net addition of carbon dioxide into the atmosphere.

Already 14% of the world's energy comes from biomass, primarily from burning wood.[209] The drawback to getting much of our energy from trees is that growing them requires enormous amounts of land. There is an alternative biomass material that, if used on a massive scale, could supply much of the world's energy, using far less land, and costing far less money. This same material could also provide many other useful things to our society. What is this extraordinary plant?

HEMP

"Hemp converts the sun's energy into bio-mass more efficiently than any other plant . . . It could compete economically with petroleum-based fuels."

Alan W. Bock,
Senior columnist for the *Orange County Register*,
May 3, 1990

Hemp grows amazingly fast and could do much to help our society. It can be made into many energy-giving substances that can drive cars, provide electricity, and at the same time reduce pollution. Hemp can supply safer, cleaner, and possibly even cheaper alternatives to oil and coal.[210]

> "... *by planting six percent of the U.S. in hemp, enough oil could be produced to meet the country's energy needs.*"
>
> The Wall Street Journal, Western Edition, May 2, 1991

Hemp can do even more than give us energy. Hemp fibers produce the highest quality and longest lasting paper ever made.[211] Until 1883, hemp fibers made the majority of our world's paper.[212] Today, with our forests being destroyed for paper at a frightening rate, hemp provides a vastly preferable alternative. According to the U.S. Department of Agriculture, 10,000 acres of land planted with hemp will yield as much paper as 40,000 acres planted in trees.[213] In June of 1991, Jim Young, editor of *Pulp and Paper* magazine, wrote an editorial in which he said,

> "Hemp is the world's primary bio-mass producer, growing ten tons/acre in approximately four months. It can produce four times the amount of paper/acre that 20-year-old-trees can and will grow in all climatic zones of the contiguous 48 states."

Along with providing an excellent potential source of energy and paper, hemp can grow on an enormous diversity of terrain and be good for the land on which it grows. The anchored roots of hemp firmly hold their surroundings, preventing soil erosion and mudslides.[214] Hemp also has an extraordinary resistance to bugs, requiring no pesticides.[215] In addition, ultraviolet radiation hardly affects hemp, making it comparatively immune to the ozone layer depletion that is reducing crop yields around the world.[216]

> "Hemp, the strongest of the vegetable fibers, gives the greatest production per acre and requires the least atten-

*tion. It not only requires no weeding, but also kills off all
the weeds and leaves the soil in splendid condition for the
following crop. This, irrespective of its own monetary
value, makes it a desirable crop to grow."*

George A. Lower
Mechanical Engineering, Feb. 26, 1937

Hemp has many other uses too. While cotton uses almost half
the agricultural chemicals in the U.S.,[217] hemp rarely needs
chemicals and makes a stronger fabric than cotton.[218] An acre of
land growing hemp will produce two to three times more material
than the same land planted in cotton and serve the same pur-
poses.[219] In fact, many people say that hemp is the strongest fiber
in the world.[220] You can look up "hemp" in any encyclopedia, and
you'll most likely find that it has been used in clothes, tents, linens,
rugs, quilts, towels, rope, twine, and more. The sturdy fibers of
hemp made the first Levi's pants.[221] Hemp can also make plastic,
medicine, food, paints, and building materials.

THE HEMP STORY

The hemp plant was one of the most important crops in the
United States only a century ago. If you look at a map, you might
notice Hempstead, N.Y., Hempstead County, Ark., Hempstead,
Tex., Hemphill, N.C., and Hempfield, Pa. These regions derived
their names from their production of hemp.

George Washington, Benjamin Franklin, and Thomas
Jefferson were among thousands of Americans who cultivated the
hemp plant.[222] In fact, at one time Americans could pay their taxes
with it.[223] Our government always supported hemp production.

But in the early 1900s, as the paper industry grew, it came
to a crossroads, needing to choose between hemp and trees as its
primary source of pulp. If the hemp plant was chosen, the logging
industry would be threatened with financial ruin.[224]

William Hearst, owner of a large timber company and many
newspapers printed from tree-derived paper, started a campaign

to stop hemp.[225] He filled his newspapers with stories portraying hemp as a drug used by "criminals and minorities." Hearst used the Mexican slang word "marijuana" instead of "hemp" to help change its image from the all-American plant to an evil drug "used by minorities."[226] Hearst was joined by Du Pont and several other companies that saw a potential for profit in outlawing hemp. For Hearst and his enormous timber company, making hemp illegal was attractive because it guaranteed an enormous market for paper made from wood. For Du Pont, making hemp illegal would eliminate the stiffest competition for the company's new synthetic fabrics, such as nylon. Because of their efforts, people became afraid of this "dangerous drug," and hemp became illegal. In the process, many potential benefits to our society were also lost.

The fact that some forms of the hemp plant also produce a psychoactive substance (THC) should not blind us to the tremendous benefits this plant can provide. Hemp can be grown without any THC, making it pharmacologically inert and completely undesirable to smoke.[227]

"They (the laws that prohibit hemp) should now at least be modified to meet pending shortages of fiber, energy, and environmental quality."
Jim Young, *Pulp and Paper* magazine, June, 1991

If we legalized the use of hemp for fuel, paper, and the other valuable things it can provide our society, there would be enormous benefits to the Earth and all generations to come. The youth of today are the policymakers of tomorrow. Our generation has the opportunity to make the changes that our future demands. Let's do it.

MORE HUMANS EQUALS MORE PROBLEMS

Through our use of products, our food choices, and our energy choices, we hold the future in our hands. There is hope. We all have the opportunity to make a positive difference by greatly reducing our negative impact on the Earth.

No matter how well we use our resources, however, the Earth has its limits. Even if we all become vegetarians, use solar energy, ban cars, eat organically grown food, and recycle everything, there are limits to how many of us the Earth can sustain. As more people join this planet, many problems become harder to solve. With every new human, more products will be consumed and discarded, more food will be grown and eaten, more houses will be built, and more energy will be used.

"In the 6 seconds it takes you to read this sentence, 24 people will be added to the Earth's population ... Within an hour, (that number will reach) 11,000. By day's end ... 260,000.

Before you go to bed two nights from now, the net growth in human numbers will be enough to fill a city the size of San Francisco.

It took four million years for humanity to reach the 2 billion mark. Only 30 years to add a third billion. And now we're increasing by 95 million every single year.

No wonder they call it the human race."

Paul Ehrlich, *Zero Population Growth*

The Population Explosion

Population in Billions

2025 — 8.6 billion[232]

1993 — 5.5 billion[231]

1950 — 2.5 billion[230]

1850 — 1 billion[229]

1 AD — 250 million[228]

Limiting population growth may be one of the most critical issues we face as we strive to preserve our resources. What can we, as young people, do about the population explosion?

For one thing, we can take responsibility for our lives so that we don't accidentally add to it. Every year, nearly 13 million teenagers become parents.[233] We are the age group that typically has the least economic stability, and therefore the hardest time raising children. In addition, almost half of the pregnancies that occur in our age group are unplanned. [234]

To create a positive future for ourselves and our world, we'll need to have fewer babies and safer sex, and realize that being a parent is a sacred responsibility. We'll also need to consider our global situation before deciding to bring another person into this world.

When we take responsibility for how we express our sexuality, we can turn one of the most personal things we do into an act of compassion for the future of life.

CHAPTER TEN

THE TROPICAL RAINFORESTS

"You can't solve a problem on the same level that it was created."

Albert Einstein, scientist and philosopher

So far, we've looked at how our consumer, food, and energy choices affect the future of life on Earth. We've learned about powerful actions we can take and clear choices we can make. And yet, simply knowing what we need to do may not be enough. The solutions are clear, but without a change in attitude, the human race may continue to create its own destruction. In the remaining chapters, we will learn more about environmental issues, and we will also explore new ways of being and relating to the world. As humans, we are the biggest threat our planet faces, and also the greatest hope. In every moment, with our attitudes and actions, we create the future. Sometimes, the impact is felt thousands of miles away . . . .

We're walking slowly through a celebration of life. From every direction we hear the sounds of birds, monkeys, frogs, insects, and rushing water, joining in a magical chorus. Nearby, a butterfly with a 12-inch wingspan flutters past, searching for a tasty flower. Thousands of flowering plants surround us. Trees tower over our heads, but even when we look up we can hardly see them, because they're covered by every kind and color of plant. Some of the vines that travel 130 feet down from the tallest branches are as wide as a human body.

We've now walked a mile. In that time, we've passed 200 species of trees, 150 kinds of birds, 50 types of butterflies, 30 species of reptiles, dozens of amphibious creatures, and a greater variety of insects than we could ever count. Some of the leaves we've passed are six feet long. All of them are covered by a constant flow of warm, dripping water.

We are in a tropical rainforest. Forests like this cover less than six percent of the land on our globe, but house more than half of our world's plant and animal species,[235] and contain 80% of the Earth's land vegetation.[236]

WHY ARE THEY CALLED TROPICAL "RAINFORESTS"?

Let's put it this way: You probably wouldn't need to take regular showers if you lived in one. If you consider that New York City averages 43 inches of rain per year and San Francisco averages 23 inches, while a tropical rainforest receives between *140* and *400* inches of rain every year, you'll understand where the rainforests get their name.[237] And just like a shower, tropical rainforests are hot—many of them average 80°F.[238] This unique combination of a constantly warm, tropical climate and year-round rain makes tropical rainforests a perfect home for an enormous diversity of plants and animals.

FOODS THAT COULD FEED US

"And then there is food. Thousands of tropical (rainforest) plants have edible parts, and some are superior to our most common crops. There are thought to be many plants that can be developed for commercial use, creating foods to feed a hungry world."

John Elkington, Julia Hailes, and Joel Makower,
The Green Consumer

In the rainforest, there are approximately 2,500 tropical fruits that people could eat. Of these, only about 15 are available commercially in the U.S.[239] Plants that people first found in the rainforest include rice, coffee, tea, chocolate, lemons, oranges, bananas, pineapples, corn, potatoes, tomatoes, peanuts, avocados, cashews, and vanilla.[240]

The winged bean, which grows in the rainforests of New Guinea, has been called a "one-species supermarket." Why? Because the entire plant—including roots, seeds, stems, leaves, and flowers—is edible. Nutritious and tasty, the winged bean grows fast—reportedly reaching a height of 15 feet in a few weeks.[241] And there are still many valuable foods that we have yet to discover.

MEDICINES THAT COULD HEAL US

"The drug that saved (my daughter's) life was derived from a plant called the rosy periwinkle. The rosy periwinkle was native to the island country of Madagascar. The irony is that ninety percent of the forested area of Madagascar has been destroyed. We are losing entire genetic stocks of wild living resources at a time when we're learning about the potential medical marvels of some of these plants, like the one used to cure my daughter. We are destroying them and their potential values forever. This is a tragedy with incredible consequences to the future of global societies."

Jay D. Hair, President
The National Wildlife Federation

Medicines (vincristine and vinblastine) that are derived from the rosy periwinkle now give us an 80% chance of curing childhood leukemia, when just a few years ago only 20% of the children who got the disease survived.[242] Other drugs derived from rainforest flowers help cure Hodgkin's Disease.[243] In fact, half of the active ingredients in the drugs and pharmaceuticals bought in the United States were originally discovered in wild plants.[244] Because tropical rainforests house so many of the Earth's plant species, they also contain many medicines that could help or cure people with illnesses.

> *"Wild (plant) species in tropical forests and other natural habitats are among the most important resources available to humankind, and so far they are the least utilized."*
> Edward O. Wilson, *Scientific American*

Humans have studied less than one percent of the plants in tropical rainforests.[245] From this small percentage we have found plants that save lives every day. If we were to thoroughly study the rainforest plants, we might find cures to some of the diseases that plague us. But if we lose the tropical rainforests, we lose this possibility. There's no way to know how many of us may die needlessly with every plant species driven to extinction.

> *"Fifty to one hundred species will become extinct every day during the next 20 years. Most of them are found in the tropics, and most will never have been studied or collected. Who knows what invaluable medicines are contained in plants we'll never even know existed?"*
> Brian Boom, New York Botanical Garden

THE NATIVES OF THE LAND

When the rainforests disappear, we lose more than the animals, plants, and medicines in them. We also lose the people who have lived there for thousands of years.

Now we're watching a tribe of native people in the Amazon rainforest. We see one of the tribesmen walking through the forest, but we can't hear him, because he's almost silent. He stops suddenly with a smile on his face, noticing a tree just ahead. This is the medicine he's been looking for. The tree has spirals of bark starting to peel off. With extraordinary care, he scrapes off some of the bark without harming the tree, and carries it back to his tribe, where a three-year-old girl is dangerously ill. Red bumps cover her body from head to toe, she has a high fever, and her neck is swollen. The child's mother waits patiently for the medicine man to prepare a remedy with the medicinal bark. After a few minutes, he has made it into a tea, and he serves it to the three-year-old girl, who will soon be healthy again.

Elsewhere in the village, one of the tribal mothers smells the air and senses that today is the day to plant 13 of the tribes' 46 crops. Throughout the planting process, as in everything they do, this tribe is careful to respect and cherish the environment around them. Their culture has lived here for thousands of years. Their way of living is built around making sure that all future generations can have the same clean and healthy environment that they have had. With each succeeding generation, the knowledge vital to the preservation of the Earth and its people gets passed on. The indigenous people are the original environmentalists; we have much to learn from them.

These peoples use techniques that allow them to survive in the rainforest without depleting their natural surroundings.[246] They practice truly sustainable agriculture.

"Their cultures should command our respect by virtue of the fact that they are sustainable, something our 'educated' Western culture has yet to attain."
Scott Lewis, *The Rainforest Book*

Rainforest tribes can teach us about medicinal and edible plants. The Lua tribe in Northern Thailand can grow 75 different food crops and 21 different medicinal plants.[247] The Hanunoo people in the Philippines have developed 430 rainforest crops.[248]

Indigenous peoples can also teach us about farming and irrigation methods, about ways to protect crops without using poisonous pesticides, and—perhaps most importantly—they can lead us to a sense of reverence and respect for the world in which we all live.

"Nature is to be respected. All life and every single living being is to be respected. That's the only answer."
Rolling Thunder, a modern medicine man

Native peoples depend on the forest for their survival. As the forest is being destroyed, so are these people from whom we could learn so much. Much as the spread of Western civilization in the 18th and 19th centuries killed off many Native Americans, the destruction of the tropical rainforests is wiping out many more indigenous tribes today.

> *"If they continue to extract logs and timber from our forest, our lives will wither like leaves on the trees, like fish without water."*
>
> Along Sega, the Penan Tribe, Malaysia

Between six and nine million people once lived in the tropical rainforests of the Amazon basin. Now, fewer than 200,000 remain,[249] and the number is declining rapidly. Rainforest destruction has completely exterminated at least 90 different tribes in Brazil alone.[250] We are destroying cultures from whom we could learn so much and gaining ignorance we may never shed.

EVERY SINGLE SECOND

> *"We have probed the Earth, excavated it, burned it, ripped things from it, buried things in it, chopped down its forests, leveled its hills, muddied its waters and dirtied its air. That does not fit my definition of a good tenant. If we were here on a month-to-month basis, we would have been evicted long ago."*
>
> Rose Bird, Former Chief Justice
> California Supreme Court

It took up to 100 million years for the tropical rainforests to evolve.[251] It has taken only 40 years to destroy more than half of them.[252] Every second, a football field-sized chunk of lush tropical rainforest is gone forever;[253] every year, we lose another 20 million acres.[254] Tropical rainforests once covered 14% of the land on our globe.[255] But because of pressure from industry, consumerism, and greed, tropical rainforests now cover less then six percent of the

Earth's land.[256] Destroying the rest of our rainforests could be one of the most tragic mistakes in the history of human existence.

In every acre of rainforest that's destroyed, huge numbers of plants and animals die too. Any one of them could be the last of its kind. If the current rate of rainforest destruction continues, between 1990 and the year 2000, our forest practices may have caused up to a million species of animals and plants to be extinguished forever.[257] While the extinction of some species is a natural occurrence, it is now happening 10,000 times faster than it did before the appearance of human beings.[258]

"As the forests vanish, part of life's richness is slowly lost, acre by acre, day by day."
                                    Scott Lewis, *The Rainforest Book*

Most of a tropical rainforest's minerals and nutrients are stored in its trees and plants, not in the ground. When we cut or burn the forest, there are no roots left to hold the soil together. When the heavy rains come, the soil washes away. What happens then?

Let's take a trip back to the rainforest we saw a brief time ago. We're walking slowly along the same mile of Earth we visited. But things are a little different now. The only sound we hear is our own footsteps. Where there used to be dense foliage, vibrant flowers, and a spectacular abundance of life in full bloom, now only a few blades of grass and burnt tree stumps poke out of this barren wasteland. The rain starts to fall again, but it no longer drops from leaf to leaf, sustaining thousands of forms of life. Now the water slams into the Earth, picking up bits of soil as it pours into the streams, polluting them with the dirt it has gathered.

The plants and trees that once thrived in these lands are gone. The tens of thousands of animal species that once lived here are gone too, and in their place are cows.

THE BEEF AGAINST RAINFOREST BEEF

Rainforests are often cut down or burned so that cattle can be brought in to graze. As they chew up the grass that tries to grow on the deforested land, their hooves stomp on and wipe out the last of the vegetation. Soon the land is no longer suitable even for grazing cattle. Then the ranchers move further into the rainforest, cut down more trees, and the stomping and chewing starts all over again. This is the process that has already destroyed much of the rainforests in Latin America.[259] In 1960, 130,000 square miles of these thriving forests covered Central America. Today, less than half of that remains.[260]

> *"It stretches the imagination to conceive how fast the timeless rainforests of Central America have been destroyed so people can have seemingly cheap hamburgers."*
>
> John Robbins, *Diet For A New America*

When we eat rainforest beef, we don't pay the whole price at the cash register. Every four ounces (an average hamburger) is responsible for the destruction of 55 square feet of tropical rainforest, the loss of 1,000 pounds of vegetation, and the death of between 20 and 30 forms of life.[261]

When we choose to eat less (or no) rainforest beef, we are making a powerful choice for the rainforests.

TIMBER!

The United States is the world's number one importer of processed tropical timber.[262] We look at teak, mahogany, and other rainforest hardwoods almost every day in the doors, tables, desks, bookshelves, houses, and sometimes even the paper we buy. The developed world's huge demand for exotic timber is wiping out tropical rainforests all over the world. In most cases oak, fir, maple, or pine can be grown locally and sustainably, costing us less money.

As consumers, we can avoid tropical wood products such as rosewood, teak, and mahogany.

'DEVELOPMENT'

Highways, dams, and mines all play leading roles in destroying our forests. Highways give access to people who want to clear the forests. One highway in Rondonia and Matto Grossa has led to the destruction of 20% of the rainforests in its sur-rounding area.[263]

Dams flood huge areas of land, displace indigenous peoples, and wipe out wildlife, all for quick and seemingly cheap energy. Many of these dams are worthless after only ten years because the soil erosion caused by tropical deforestation leads to huge amounts of silt building up at the bottom of the dams, eventually clogging them.

Underneath the rainforests lie gold, oil, coal, and other precious materials. Miners destroy rainforests to have better access to these resources. The chemicals used by miners to separate gold from raw ore contaminate streams and rivers, and poison the people who drink water downstream.

(You can send a letter to the president of the World Bank, urging him to stop financing rainforest dams and instead, fund small-scale projects that benefit rainforests and their inhabitants. See the address on page 165. To adopt your own acre of the rainforest, contact the Protect-an-Acre Program, page 161.)

WHO IS RESPONSIBLE FOR RAINFOREST DESTRUCTION?

We can blame certain multi-national corporations, who take advantage of the situation and see an opportunity to make some quick bucks. Or we can point our fingers at the people whose actual hands are on the chain saws. Many of these people, driven by hunger and poverty, destroy the forests because it is their only hope of making enough money to survive (usually with cattle or mining). But one thing is certain: We all become infinitely poorer when we lose our rainforests.

The destruction of our rainforests is too complex to blame on one person or one company, on one industry or one government. It has its roots in a way of relating to the world. Many of us live in environments created by and designed for humans. Because of this, we may come to believe that the world is made for us. We may come to value trees only for their wood, and paper and animals only for their meat, milk, or eggs.

Some people are beginning to see that this attitude doesn't work. They are realizing that the Earth is a community in which we are participants, not a commodity to use and destroy. As individuals change how they see the world, the solutions begin to emerge. Sometimes the solutions are even better economically.

A recent study by the World Wildlife Fund showed that Brazilians could make between three and 100 times more money from a properly managed rainforest than by current methods which destroy the forests.[264] A well-managed forest will provide an on-going source of valuable goods and money, whereas cattle, mining, dams, and timber make the land only valuable for a brief time, after which it becomes worthless. Properly managing a forest includes the sustainable harvesting of things like Brazil nuts, cashews, rubber, resins, and wild tropical fruits, ecological tourism, and more.

In our attitude towards the rainforests, as with so many issues humanity faces, we have many choices. We can choose to think and act for short-term financial profit or for the long-term survival of life on Earth. Even though our rainforests are confronted with enormous problems, we're lucky. Why? Because we still have enormous rainforests to explore, mountains to climb, a great diversity of species to discover and protect, and many priceless jewels of nature to preserve. And we have something else that we might not have a few years from now: time. If we act now, we still have the time to create the changes we want. Let's use it.

CHAPTER ELEVEN

THE CHOICE FOR PEACE

Let's talk about war. No, not the card game, the activity where people try as hard as possible to clobber each other. Many of us believe that having a strong military to defend our country is worth any environmental and human sacrifices it may cause. Many of us also feel that national security should come at any cost, because it prevents us from being brutally invaded by other countries. And to many people, the purpose behind having a strong military and fighting wars is to create peace. As former President George Bush said during the Persian Gulf war, *"The goal of the war is peace."*

Don't know about you, but there just might be a better path to peace than killing people.

War is mass murder—the systematic extermination of the enemy. But war doesn't just take place in the battlefield. As we will see in this chapter, the mentality of war is the same attitude that is behind genocide, racism, gang violence, and verbal, as well as physical, abuse. As history has shown us, this is not an attitude that leads to peace. Tribes, gangs, races, religions, and nations have consistently attacked each other, killing hundreds of millions of people. For thousands of years, there has been no world peace.

Every war that has ever taken place has shared the same battleground: Earth. Every bomb dropped and every bullet fired

128

has taken an enormous toll not just in human lives, but also on our environment and our shared future. So long as wars continue, there can never be environmental sanity.

AT WAR WITH OURSELVES

"We are in the business of protecting the nation, not the environment."
U.S. Military Base Commander in Virginia[265]

Lorraine Hufstutler of Mountainview, New Mexico, lives in the shadow of Kirtland Air Force Base. Her feelings about the nearby base are far from positive. Why? Hazardous wastes are traveling off base, contaminating the community's water supply.[266]

"We can no longer grow our gardens, we can no longer safely bathe, and we have no water to drink."
Lorraine Hufstutler

Thousands of cities and towns across the United States and countless communities in the rest of the world, share these problems.[267] In the early 1990s, the U.S. military generated between 400,000 and 500,000 tons of toxics every year—more than the top five U.S. chemical companies combined.[268]

"The world's armed forces are quite likely the single largest polluter on Earth ... Military toxics are contaminating water used for drinking or irrigation, killing fish, befouling the air, and rendering vast tracts of land unusable for generations to come."
Michael Renner, Worldwatch Institute
State of the World 1991

Many of the world's military forces now have at their disposal one of the greatest threats our world has ever known: nuclear weapons. As many of us know, if they are ever used in sufficient quantity, they could destroy all life on Earth many times over. And even if a nuclear war never happens, people are already dying.

Between 1945 and 1989, more than 1,800 nuclear bombs were exploded around the world in tests. The radiation released in the process is said to have caused 86,000 birth defects and some 150,000 premature deaths.[269] Countless others have been killed by the nuclear waste created to produce these weapons.

The world's military forces also use up large chunks of land and energy. If you put together the world's militarily-owned land, it would occupy a space bigger than California and Texas combined.[270] The world's military forces burn more fossil fuels than Japan, the world's second largest economy.[271]

Making, testing, and using weapons is far from friendly to the environment. Under the banner of "national security," military forces are often free from environmental regulations.[272] The Research Institute for Peace Policy in Germany estimates that *20% of all global environmental degradation is caused by the military and its activities.*[273] Not only that, . . .

IT'LL COST YA'

"Every gun that is made, every warship launched, every rocket fired, signifies . . . in the final sense a theft from those who hunger and are not fed, those who are cold and are not clothed."

Dwight D. Eisenhower, former President of the United States

Even in times of peace, military forces are preparing for war. In 1992, with the Berlin wall gone, 46 years of conflict with the Soviet Union over, and much of eastern Europe sweeping towards democracy, the United States was still spending $34 billion every year on keeping troops and planes ready for war in Europe.[274]

In this same year, the world spent about $900 billion on military operations.[275] It's been justified because countries want to have a strong army just in case they get into a war. So they keep

The Biggest Military Forces

on Earth[276]

Military Spending by U.S. and Its "Presumed Allies" *		Military Spending by "Potential Adversaries" of the U.S.*	
Country	Spending (billions)	Country	Spending (billions)
U.S.	$291	Iraq[3]	$9
Japan	$40	Iran[2]	$6
France	$36	North Korea	$6
United Kingdom	$35	Syria[2]	$3
Germany	$31	Libya[3]	$2
Italy	$17	Cuba[1]	$1
Canada	$10	**Total Potential Adversaries**	**$27**
South Korea	$12	**Military Spending by "Other Large Militaries"** *	
Netherlands	$7	Russia	$29
Spain	$7	China[1]	$22
Australia	$7	India[2]	$8
Turkey	$5	Pakistan	$3
Belgium, Denmark, Greece, Norway, Portugal	$14 (total)	Vietnam[1]	$2
Total U.S. & Presumed Allies	**$512**	**Total Other Large Militaries**	**$64**
All data 1993 except: [1]1992 [2]1991 [3]1990 - *Pentagon Classifications			

spending more money on their military forces, trying to outdo each other. And so do their potential enemies. With each dollar spent, the destructive potential of the human race increases, and with it, people's fear of war.

Where does our government get $291 billion a year to spend on the military? From our taxes. In 1993, 47 cents out of every income tax dollar the U.S. government spent went to the military.[277]

We, as humans, have enormous capacity for intelligence, wisdom, and creativity. We have the remarkable ability to invent things that otherwise never would have existed. We are gifted with human emotions that enable us to cry, to celebrate, and to care passionately about others. We have the willpower that lets us persevere in the face of obstacles. Each of us is a miracle.

Every one of us has something unique and precious we can contribute to the unfolding of life on Earth. But in many ways, the human race isn't utilizing its talents, creativity, and resources for the betterment of all life. In fact, much of the world's energy goes towards the ability to fight wars. The military is the biggest industry in the world. In 1990, the world's military forces employed more than 45 million people.[278]

"If someone has the power to wound or heal, you look to them to have the moral depth and vision to use that power to heal."

Douglas du Charme
relief worker after the Persian Gulf war

What would happen if our governments shifted their focus and the way they spend money? Could we end starvation? Is it possible that we could end air pollution and smog? Many people think so.

THE SHIFT TO ENVIRONMENTAL SANITY

"The amount of money necessary to reverse the world's most pressing environmental problems is estimated to be only one-sixth of current world military spending."

The Worldwatch Institute

If our taxes stopped paying our brilliant scientists to develop bigger and more destructive bombs, our taxes could pay these same scientists to figure out how to stop global warming and ozone layer depletion. Considering the amazing ingenuity and creativity of humans, many of our environmental problems could become things of the past. We could fight each other less and help each other more.

"The ability of (the world's military forces) to clothe, feed, train, deploy, and command groups of people is unmatched. It is the only organization, potential or actual, that has the capacity to address environmental problems on the scale that they exist."

Gary Zukav, *The New Mission of the Military: The Military And The Environment*

The military's job is to protect the people from their enemies. The environmental crisis could be the biggest enemy we face. Imagine if the air force was in charge of fighting air pollution and smog. The navy could protect the dolphins, whales, and other creatures living in the seas. The army and marines could care for the land and do whatever else they could to ensure a safe world for future generations.

This wouldn't mean an end to military defense. There could still be armed forces to protect our countries, but many troops could be freed up to help secure a positive future.

OUR EARTH: AN OPPORTUNITY FOR PEACE

"There's no such thing as a winnable war."

"Russians," a song by Sting

No matter which side is being attacked, we are all victims of war. The Persian Gulf war of 1990 led to burning oil fields which blackened the sky over much of the Middle East and contributed to global warming. The sky has no borders. The largest oil spill in world history poured into the Persian Gulf during that war. The ocean has no borders, either. Fundamentally, we are all interconnected, sharing the same planet upon which all of our lives depend. As one astronaut wrote,

"The first day or so, we all pointed to our countries. The third or fourth day, we were pointing to our continents. By the fifth day, we were aware of only one Earth."

Sultan Bin Salman al-Saud
The Kingdom of Saudi Arabia

We all breathe the same air, and we all drink the same water. The environment is something we all have in common. When we realize that everyone alive shares the same planet, a great opportunity arises: the chance to join forces, healing the world for which we all care. There's no way any one person or any one country can turn our environmental crisis around. This task can best be accomplished if the nations and races of the Earth can learn to peacefully work together.

WHERE DOES WORLD PEACE START?

Have you ever seen someone demonstrating for peace whose attitude was anything but peaceful? Many people participate in the hostile attitudes that lead to war, even as they seek to wage peace.

"The fellow was holding a peace sign that he carried in the protest line. He got in some kind of argument with a bystander and ended up hitting the other person over the head with his peace sign."

Maria Gomez, Santa Cruz, Cal.

Many of us (even people working for peace) can unknowingly have the attitudes that create conflict. Let's suppose for a moment that you, the reader, are the chief executive officer (CEO) of a company that is causing environmental pollution. And let's suppose that you are meeting with an angry citizen who believes that the local community has been polluted by your company. Let's suppose this is what you hear.

"You are destroying the planet! Your company has killed thousands of people, and you don't even care. You must be a heartless person to be able to commit such ruthless crimes. How can you live with yourself?! You don't care about me, you don't care about the people in my community, you don't care about the animals you're killing, and you probably don't even care about the children's future. All you care about is money. You're greedy! You deserve to take a bath in your own toxic waste!"

Supposing you really were the CEO of this company, what would these comments make you want to do? Would you feel open-minded or defensive towards what you just heard? Would this meeting be likely to lead towards positive changes?

Now let's try the meeting again with a different approach. This time you hear,

"I'm concerned about the state of our world and I hope you are too. I'm concerned that some of the things your company is doing might be making things worse. Would you be willing to look at this with me? I'm here to create more understanding. There's been a 43% increase in cancer in this community since your company started up here. Some doctors believe this increase is partly caused by your company's toxic waste. Many people are upset. People are scared for all the animals who are dying.

People are frightened for our children's future. I've come here today to learn about your perspectives and to see if there's any way I can help you be a leader in environmental protection. It's people like you who could lead the way towards an improved environment."

How would this approach make you, as the company's CEO, feel? Would you be more or less open-minded or defensive than in the first meeting? Which would probably have the most positive long-term results?

Many of us will agree that the second meeting would be more effective than the first one. Perhaps the most important feature of this meeting was the positive focus, acknowledging and appreciating the CEO for her/his good side and envisioning how the CEO could be a participant in creating a better world, rather than putting him/her down for not already doing more.

Whether we're destroying or helping the environment, it affects all of us. Some people take longer than others to realize the urgency of the environmental crisis. As we saw in the second meeting, by respecting the people we want to reach, we can better help them to become open to our message.

In the first meeting with the CEO, we saw an example of how the mentality of war perpetuates itself. The attitudes that lead to war and peace aren't just present in certain meetings with CEOs. They occur in many other aspects of our lives: in our families and in our countries, in our relationships, and in our neighborhoods.

Let's suppose there's a conflict between Herman and Hilda. Because they realize that conflicts often arise when people don't feel heard or understood, they decide to "mirror" each other. They start by sitting, facing each other. They decide that Hilda will go first, so she then expresses what she wants Herman to know. Herman listens as carefully as he can, without responding. Hilda might say,

"I can't stand the smell of your feet. So far today, I've almost passed out three times. It's not that you're a bad person. In fact, I think you're kinda' cool. I just have a really sensitive nose. I'd appreciate it if you'd have some respect for the people around you by wearing clean socks."

When Hilda is finished, Herman "mirrors" her, repeating the important points that Hilda expressed as best he remembers them. For example,

"You don't like the smell of my feet. You want me to wash them all day. You've almost passed out three times today. You've got a sensitive nose, and you don't like me."

Then Hilda shares again whatever Herman missed. For example:

"You got most of it, but you left out a few things. First of all, I think you're a cool person. It's not that I don't like you—I just don't like how your feet smell. I never wanted you to wash your feet all day; I just want you to wear clean socks."

Then Herman "mirrors" back what he left out the first time. If needed, they will continue this process until Hilda feels fully heard. Then Herman has a chance to speak, and Hilda "mirrors" him. If they feel it is appropriate, they can do more than one round of "mirroring."

Consciously "mirroring" another person or taking time to reiterate what you hear them saying can be a significant step in resolving conflicts. But no technique is as important as basic human goodwill and the willingness to forgive.

Let's take a look at South Central Los Angeles. Two gangs, (let's suppose their names are the "52nd Rollers" and the "Broadway Bomb Squad") live in bordering neighborhoods. One evening, a member of the 52nd Rollers, Mike, goes into the Broadway Bomb Squad's territory and gets shot. Mike's fellow 52nd Rollers mourn his death and swear they'll take revenge in his honor. The next night, two of the 52nd Rollers that Mike grew up with sneak into the Broadway Bomb Squad's territory in the middle of the night and kill three of them. Two days later, while the 52nd Rollers are hanging out, they are interrupted by rapid gunfire as members of the Broadway Bomb Squad take some revenge of their own. Four more 52nd Rollers see their lives slip away. And so it goes, until most of the original gang members are dead.

"An eye for an eye will only leave the whole world blind."
Mahatma Gandhi

Ironically, all of these people wanted their gangs to survive and prosper. Each death was mourned by family and friends. But the deaths continued to mount, as the mentality of war perpetuated itself. If these two gangs had been able to make peace, their members would have been much more likely to survive.

"The best way to destroy an enemy is to make him (or her) a friend."
Abraham Lincoln

Each of us has stereotypes and judgments about other groups of people that we have picked up at some point in our lives. These can take hold deep in our minds and color our perceptions even when we do not consciously believe them. Breaking free of prejudice barriers can be a challenging process. Few of us are conscious of all the pain, separation, and violence that stem from lumping a diverse group of people under a common, stereotyped umbrella. At its most extreme, prejudice can lead to cultural genocide, such as the on-going onslaught against Native Americans.

Every single human being is different. To stereotype others robs us of the opportunity to appreciate the unique talents and gifts each individual brings to the world. When we become aware of our stereotypes, we can begin to release them and more fully enjoy the individuality of every living being. In time, the diversity of the human race might be something we can come to appreciate rather than fear.

Because the environmental crisis affects all of us, turning it around will take all of us. In it, there is an opportunity we've never before had, an opportunity for individuals, races, religions, and nations to play their own unique role in creating a more healthy and peaceful world.

"We must learn to live together as brothers, or we are going to perish together as fools."

Reverend Martin Luther King, Jr.

Learning to live together with less fear and hate, and more peace and friendship, is no easy task. But the process starts when we decide we want to, and the whole world reaps the benefits of that decision.

Tens of thousands of years of clobbering each other is enough. If the people of the world can learn to work together while cherishing each other's uniqueness, we may yet have world peace.

CHAPTER TWELVE

THE CHOICE TO BE A WARRIOR FOR THE EARTH

> "If today is a typical day on planet Earth, we will lose 116 square miles of rainforest or about an acre a second. We will lose another 72 square miles to encroaching deserts, the result of human mismanagement and overpopulation. We will lose 40-100 species, and no one knows whether the number is 40 or 100. Today the human population will increase by 250,000. And today we will add 2,700 tons of CFCs to the atmosphere and 15 million tons of carbon. Tonight the Earth will be a little hotter, its waters more acidic, and the fabric of life more threadbare."
>
> David W. Orr, Professor of Environmental Studies
> Oberlin College, Oberlin, Ohio, 1990

We are in danger. Our environmental problems are growing and taking lives. Sometimes the problems can be so big that they feel overwhelming. As a result, many of us go through times of feeling depressed, of giving up, of believing that human life is doomed.

Our generation lives without knowing if life on Earth has a future. A nuclear shadow hangs over our heads, the ozone layer is thinning, our air is filling with smog, and people are living in fear. What does this do to us? How do we feel, being a part of the species that is creating ecological catastrophe?

HOW DO WE RESPOND?

Let's suppose we try to ignore the world's problems. We don't want to think about the 15 million children who die of malnutrition every year or about the hundreds of thousands of Americans who live on the streets without homes. We want to have fun, not get bummed out.

We believe that ignorance is bliss, and our motto is, "What I don't know about can't hurt me." We dismiss the environmental crisis, because we think that it will only interrupt our enjoyment of life. We protect ourselves behind a "comfortable" wall of denial.

Now let's suppose that we are walking along a busy street in a big city. Ahead of us, a homeless man holds a cup in the air, hoping somebody will put in some change. This man makes us feel uncomfortable. As we hurry past him, we pretend that he isn't there. Our body, however, feels his presence. Our denial enables us to pretend we weren't bothered, but inside, we are affected.

We pass the homeless man without relating to him. We don't want to think about him, because it may bring us pain. Later, our lungs hurt from the foul air. But we pretend we're fine. A few more bricks add to our wall of denial.

The process of denial becomes a routine in our daily life. We learn about war and we try to push what we've learned out of our consciousness. We're told that the beef we eat causes heart attacks, and we ignore the facts. We hear about our polluted environment, and we go on driving a gas guzzler.

This process continues until we are psychically numb. Eventually, we have toughened our hearts so much that it becomes hard to feel much of anything. The road has been paved to addiction. To some of us, drugs, television, compulsive eating, and other escapist habits become more attractive.

Our goal has been to survive without letting the world's problems get us down. We have succeeded, but to master the art of denial, we've had to make some sacrifices. We have little room for compassion towards others. In fact, we may have become capable of great violence, because now we can hurt others without feeling pain. We have abandoned our conscience, and we don't even know it. Our walls of denial have become so thick and so "normal" that we are unaware of them. We've made the choice to deny.

It's a choice shared by many people. But it's not the only option.

Each of us has a natural urge, an instinct for survival, that wells up in times of danger. These are such times. Our environmental problems have become so severe that human life is now in jeopardy. Within all of our hearts, a call to action is emerging. When we listen to this call, we align ourselves with the forces of life itself. We can have the power of the mountains, the waves, the stars, and the animals behind us. We can be warriors for the Earth, acting for the survival of all life.

The problems we're facing are challenging us in many ways. They bring us face to face with our own mortality, with our uncertain future, and with the necessity to act. It takes bravery to confront this challenge and courage to stand up for our endangered future. It takes an Earth warrior.

> "The word 'warrior' comes from the Tibetan 'pawo,' which literally means one who is brave. Warriorship is the tradition of human bravery, or the tradition of fearlessness. We must be brave enough to think beyond the fire burning in the fireplace, beyond sending our children to school or getting to work in the morning. We must try to think how we can help this world."
>
> Chogyam Trungpa, *Shambhala*

The creation of a healthy future will depend on many of us having the courage to look beyond our immediate reality, to envision the world we want and to work towards our goals. It will also depend on our . . .

CONNECTION WITH THE EARTH

It can be easy for us to lose touch with the Earth. Most of us live in a human-made world of pavement, cars, machinery, carpets, televisions, and electric lights, out of touch with the elements of nature. This manufactured environment is artificial, but many of us have grown so used to it that it becomes our "real world," and nature becomes something remote. We call it the "natural world," as if it were another planet. And when we do "experience" nature, it is often on TV. Jerry Mander, founder of the Public Media Center, writes,

> "I heard many people say, 'Television is great; there are so many things on TV that we'd never otherwise experience.' People were seeing television images of Borneo forests, current events, or re-creations of historical crises, and they were believing themselves to be experiencing these places, people, and events. Yet the television image of the Borneo forest or the news or historical events was surely not the experience of them and not to be relied upon to the same extent. It was only the experience of sitting in a darkened room, staring at a flickering light, ingesting images which had been edited, cut, rearranged, sped-up, slowed down, and confined in hundreds of ways. Were people aware of the difference?"

Many of us aren't. What we watch on television may look real, but it can't possibly compare to the feeling of walking through a forest, of hearing the sounds of animals and wind, or of the mystery and wonder that nature provides. If we believe that an image of nature is equal to or even similar to the experience of nature and are satisfied enough with the image that we don't seek out the real experience, nature is in big trouble, and so are we.

. . . The average American watches more than five hours of television every day . . .

Television jumps from one camera angle to another many times every minute. In ads, the jumps are even faster, sometimes many per second. At one moment, we can be watching a beach in the Bahamas, and at the next moment, we may be watching a car chase in New York. The television's images are constantly on the move, designed to capture and keep our attention by any means necessary. Compared to television's fast pace, the deep rhythms of nature can appear slow and boring. When we're artificially stimulated, it may be hard to slow down enough to contact our world and ourselves in any depth.

The less we are in touch with our planet's natural beauty, the more we separate ourselves from the Earth community. In this separation, we can be participants in environmental destruction without even knowing it.

. . . We spend one-third of our waking lives mesmerized by television's electronic glow . . .

Many of us watch TV because "there's nothing else to do." But there's a planet to save, and we've got plenty of things to do. If enough of us stop zoning out on TV and other escapist habits and take action for a healthy future, we just might turn things around.

We can start weaving ourselves back into the web of life by venturing into the pristine wilderness of the Earth. We can swim in pure lakes, climb tall mountains, hike through deep forests, pick wild berries, or go camping. We can find a spot of nature, no matter how large or small, and enjoy it to the fullest. We can also share these beautiful natural areas with our friends and family.

To be a warrior for the Earth, we need to know what we're protecting. We also need to be humble enough to open to and learn from the powerful forces of the Earth. They can be supports and allies in our quest for a healthy future.

HAVING A POSITIVE ATTITUDE

Here is a guy who wants to work for social change, but he never seems to be successful. He's got the best of intentions, but things never seem to work out. Perhaps it has something to do with the fact that he:

* notices what's wrong with any situation
* dwells on how awful it will be if things don't work out
* uses potential problems as an excuse for apathy
* stops and goes no further after making a mistake
* looks for reasons not to act
* finds fault with others as an excuse to avoid improving the situation

In contrast, here is a young woman. She also wants to be a warrior for the Earth, but she is effective; people respond positively to her. Maybe it's because she:

* appreciates herself and others for good things that are accomplished
* holds a positive vision of how the future could be
* acts to create what she wants
* tries with renewed creativity after making a mistake
* persists until the task is finished
* has the courage to be the first person to do something
* is confident in herself
* is willing to dream and to believe that miracles are possible

It's pretty rare for anyone to always have a positive or negative attitude. But in every moment and in every situation, we can choose how we want to relate to what surrounds us. Every time we choose to have a positive attitude, our world can become a little healthier and happier, and our dreams can come a little closer to reality.

HOLDING A VISION

"Where there is no vision, the people perish . . . "
Proverbs, 29:18

Many of us know what we don't want; maybe we're fighting rainforest destruction or racism or something else. We know what we're against, but do we know what we're for? As warriors for the Earth, it's crucial that we consider what we're working towards. The more we can get in touch with our sense of purpose, the more it can be fulfilled. When we envision what we want, when we have a positive goal to work towards, solutions become possible.

Here is one possible vision of a future that might come to be . . . .

In a grocery store in a busy city, everything comes from bulk bins, with no wasted packaging. The food is organic, grown in soil that is conserved for future generations. Outside the store, people are walking in the shade down a tree-lined street. Others are bicycling or driving cars fueled by the power of the sun.

The air is clean and the water is pure. Birth and death rates have slowed, and starvation is a thing of the past.

Beyond the city, we can see the rest of the lands of the Earth. Everywhere, life is abundant. In dense, mysterious rainforests, on hot African savannas, in the old-growth forests, and great open prairies of North America, the land is thriving with all forms of life.

At the edge of the land, waves wash back from clean beaches into the ocean. Dolphins leap into the air and return underwater, where a closer look reveals colorful coral and flashing schools of fish. If we could look even closer, we would see the tiny phytoplankton that, protected by the Earth's ozone shield, produce more oxygen for life on this planet than even the vast forests that cover much of the land.

The Earth provides a stable climate and generous harvests. Humans no longer exploit animals. People still remember the environmental and social problems of the past and feel great pride to have made so many needed changes.

On this planet, people have learned to honor and take care of the environment. We treat nature and each other with love and respect. All countries, ethnic groups, and religions have let go of their superficial barriers, valuing and learning from each other's unique perspectives and cooperating in creating a healthy global environment.

To many people this vision may seem impractical. *But how "realistic" is it to live without a vision?*

THE YOUTH

It's part of the youthful spirit to believe in and create what previous generations have thought to be impossible. It is this spirit that can lead the way to a positive future.

It takes courage to believe that positive change can happen. Young people have this courage. We also have energy and enthusiasm that can be channeled into effective action. We are the future. We'll be alive long enough to experience the consequences of what's being done to the environment now. Because of this, we have a great deal of motivation for creating the healthy future we deserve.

"There's an old science story . . . about the frog that's put in a pot of boiling water, and it jumps right out. Then the same frog is put in a pot of lukewarm water, and it is slowly brought to a boil. And the frog just sits there until it's rescued. . . . The frog needs a sudden contrast before it makes the connection between its danger and what it must do to save itself."

Albert Gore, Vice President of the United States, at the UNCED Conference, 1992

Youth are like frogs that have just fallen into boiling water. We feel the urgency of the environmental crisis more intensely than older people, who may have grown used to the heating water as environmental problems slowly emerged. This gives us a unique responsibility: to awaken our sleeping species. Today more than ever before, our voice needs to be heard.

GIVING OUR POWER AWAY

Many of us, as young people, find it difficult to make our voices heard. In today's society, our opinions and feelings are rarely considered. Older generations often believe that we're not complete human beings until we're "grown up." We are sometimes seen as irresponsible, idealistic, naive, or "going through a phase." Our dreams are seldom taken seriously.

There are many ways that the power of youth can be suppressed. Older generations have generally made decisions about our future without even consulting us. Parents may be too busy or too self-absorbed to really listen to what we have to offer.

Corporations, however, don't take us for granted. We are an 80 billion dollar-per-year market.[279] Many corporations give special attention to the youth market, because if a corporation can get young people to use their products, they've probably got us hooked for the rest of our lives.

> *"Today's youth are shaped by advertising . . . (they) absorb 350,000 consumptive messages before graduating from high school."*
>
> Kalle Lasn, Cat Simril, and Barbara Green
> *Adbusters* magazine

Companies with products to sell are finding new and creative ways of convincing young people to buy their products. One of the most telling of these is the growing corporate influence in our schools.

Remember the four "Basic Food Groups?" They were:

1. meat
2. dairy & eggs
3. fruits & vegetables
4. grains & beans

Have you ever wondered how they came to exist? They weren't given to Moses with the Ten Commandments.

As little kids, none of us could have imagined that the pretty charts we were shown were actually the outcome of extensive political lobbying by the huge meat and dairy industries.[280] Our teachers probably never suspected that they were being used to relay industrial propaganda, as many of them were. Our innocent and captive little minds soaked it all up like sponges. And most of us, as planned, have been willing and unquestioning consumers of vast amounts of meats and dairy products ever since.

For decades, the largest single supplier of "nutritional information" in our schools has been the National Dairy Council.[281] They have been happy to provide colorful "nutritional" materials to our schools, materials that teach us we need to eat and drink large amounts of dairy products.[282] Other commercial interests that have supported our being "educated" on the value of their products include The National Livestock & Meat Board, McDonalds, Oscar Meyer, and the Egg Board.[283] Schools, being strapped for funding, have welcomed these free materials. Corporations, eager for new customers, have welcomed the opportunity to market their products. The only people who have lost in the bargain are us, as we have been taught that half of our diet should be animal products when modern science knows this is far from the truth.

Have you ever wondered why half of all Americans die of heart disease, and yet we keep right on eating high-fat animal products? As students, we were unlikely to question what we were told. Many of us still believe it. The meat and dairy industries have been successful; they've got most of America hooked.

McDonalds and Burger King now serve their food in many school cafeterias. How many students will eat at these restaurants for the rest of their lives as a result?

"1:53 . . . 1:54 . . . Maybe a stray asteroid will come and level the school . . . 1:55 . . . 1:56 . . . 1:56 and 30 seconds . . . 31 seconds . . . 32 seconds . . . 33 seconds . . . My brain just died . . . 35 seconds . . . 36 seconds . . . I wonder if dead people are this bored . . . 38 seconds . . . 39 seconds . . . HOLD ON!!! She's rolling in a TV! No way! Hold on. It's brand new! And there's a VCR. It's shiny. I must be hallucinating!"

Nathaniel Roeg, *Big Noise Magazine*

There's a new television channel, and it's changing the way our schools operate. The arrangement is simple. Whittle Communications provides free televisions, VCRs, and satellite dishes to schools. In exchange, the schools agree to require their students to watch Channel One, a 12-minute, daily news program that Whittle produces for them.

"The programming, however, is clearly secondary to the real agenda of the Whittle Corporation's Channel One: To make a profit by selling rooms full of sedated youngsters to advertising agencies."

Dee Dee Halleck, *Lies Of Our Times*

Whittle Corporation is making millions of dollars on this deal. For every 12 minutes of daily news, there are two minutes of commercials.[284] The opportunity to bombard eight million or more captive students all at the same time attracts many corporations. Of course, it costs plenty of money. Each 30-second advertisement that a corporation buys on Channel One costs between $150,000 and $200,000.[285] But it's worth it, because we'll buy enough of their products to make the whole deal perfectly profitable. Channel One shows 600 commercials annually, and as a result, Whittle Communications makes $100 million in advertising revenue every year.[286]

Faced with ever-shrinking funds and ever more students, schools are beginning to allow increasing portions of their "educational" materials to be provided to them by corporations. For example:

- *Mobil Corporation's mock news video (called)* "Polystyrene foam and the Environment" *urges students to think of plastic as the best waste to put in landfills.*

- *Keep America Beautiful, a corporate-backed organization, defines trash incineration as 'recycling' in its curriculum.*

- *Exxon explains to kids that gasoline's 'energy value' comes from solar energy stored in its organic chemical bonds.*"

Nathaniel Roeg, Big Noise Magazine

The corporate quest to make money from the youth market affects more than sales figures. It affects the way we, as young people, feel about ourselves and our place in the world.

Marketing experts have discovered that if we can be made to feel less empowered, we will look for a sense of power and purpose outside ourselves. Advertisements teach us that feeling attractive, happy, and confident depends on what kind of car or clothing we buy and not on how we live and the kind of human beings we are. Those of us who buy into these beliefs will strive for happiness through purchasing more things.

As long as we allow ourselves to be manipulated, we will be passive consumers of products we don't need, with our minds full of beliefs that aren't really ours. Many of us lack a sense of purpose as we look outside ourselves and towards fads and styles for answers. But until we find happiness in what we do and create, and in our interactions with others, we'll never be satisfied.

THE RISING OF THE YOUTH

The 1960s were a time of turbulence, of change, and for many young people, a time of rebellion. Millions of people fiercely debated the Vietnam War, putting themselves on the line for what they believed. Many people also marched with Martin Luther King, Jr., as the civil rights movement came into full swing. There was change in the air, and the youth were leading the way. But the 1960s were also chaotic. Many youth lacked a sense of purpose, and the movement for change that had inspired many began to fizzle away.

In the 1970s, the number of active youth began to decline drastically. This trend continued through the 1980s as suicides, gang murders, and drug addiction grew in record numbers. Instead of daring to challenge how things were and working to change the world, youth began to conform without questioning. The dominant focuses in the lives of many young people had shifted from civil rights and stopping war to MTV and shopping malls. Much of the activism of the 1960s seemed to be gone.

But now the 1990s have arrived, change is in the air, and the youth are rising up again. In fact, the first few years of this decade saw a greater growth of youth activism than the U.S. has ever known.

On January 8, 1993, newspapers across the U.S. featured an article on a survey of 200,000 students that has been sponsored by UCLA researchers every year since 1966. Its findings are remarkable. In 1966, 16.3% of all high school seniors attended a political demonstration. But in 1992, the number broke all records, reaching a startling 40%. Today's youth are taking a stand for what they believe. Two-thirds of 1992's high school seniors did some kind of volunteer work, and one out of four college freshmen/women in 1993 said they planned to participate in a community action program while in college. Listen to the lyrics of some of today's music and you will hear . . .

"All the younger generations have to come to understand that the future of our nations lies within our very hands.

If we all join in together to discuss our every need we can rid this world forever of politics and greed . . .

"It's up to us, the young at heart, to give this world a brand new start.

But if we don't start today, we might as well kiss this world away . . .

"We are the young generation, and it's time that we take a stand.

We are the young, and we can make this a better land . . ."

"We Are The Young," a song by Phsycefunkapus

Young people are rising up. National polls find that 75% of the young people in the U.S. now consider the environment to be the biggest problem confronting our generation.[287] And we aren't just concerned—we're taking action.

In 1990, when the YES! Tour first went on the road, there were environmental clubs in about 20% of the schools we visited. The typical club had only ten active members. A year later, there were clubs in half of the schools, and the number of members had begun to grow. By 1994, 80% of the schools had environmental clubs, and the average number of active members had jumped to 20. This represents an eight-fold increase in student environmental activism, all in just four years.

Youth organizations working for positive change are emerging everywhere. National organizations like the Student Environmental Action Coalition (SEAC), the Environmental Youth Alliance, The SAVE Tour, Youth for Environmental Sanity (YES!), The Sierra Student Coalition, Kids For A Clean Environment (Kids' FACE), City Kids, Kids Against Pollution (KAP), and many more, all have thousands of members and are all making powerful differences in our world. Addresses and phone numbers for these groups can be found in the Appendix (pages 157-67).

THE YOUNG AT HEART

The rising of youth does not exclude people of any age. Within all of our hearts, there is the opportunity to be young, to dream, to see in new ways, and to be a warrior for the Earth.

"Youth is not a time of life; it is a state of mind. It is not a matter of rosy cheeks, red lips, and supple knees; it is a matter of the will, a quality of the imagination, a vigor of the emotions; it is the freshness of the deep springs of life.

Youth means a temperamental predominance of courage over timidity, of the appetite for adventure over the love of ease. This often exists in an adult of 60 more than a child of 20. Nobody grows old merely by a number of years. We grow old by deserting our ideals.

Years may wrinkle the skin, but to give up enthusiasm wrinkles the soul. Worry, fear, self-distrust bows the heart and turns the spirit back to dust.

Whether 60 or 16, there is in every human being's heart the lure of wonder, the unfailing, childlike appetite of what's next. In the center of your heart, and my heart there is a wireless station; so long as it receives messages of beauty, hope, cheer, courage, and power from people and from the infinite, so long are you young."

Samuel Ullman, poet and philosopher

CHOICES FOR OUR FUTURE

The time has come to raise our voices, to say YES! to a sane world for ourselves and future generations. The creatures of the oceans and forests and all other living things are crying out for us to act. Who will listen and respond to the call of the trees, the animals, and the humans who are already suffering? Who will take a stand above apathy and powerlessness? Who will show the Earth that hope is alive?

We can choose to give our power away and do nothing about the problems. We can also choose to rise above our fears to work towards a healthy future for ourselves and our children. If the hopeful ones are few, powerlessness will overcome. If the hopeful ones are strong and numerous, the power of change will be granted to all.

The choice is ours.

The time is now.

APPENDIX

YOUTH FOR ENVIRONMENTAL SANITY (YES!)

If you feel touched by the message of *Choices for Our Future*, you may be interested in YES!. We are a diverse team of youth with the common vision of creating a healthy environment. YES!, a national youth-run organization, informs, inspires, and empowers youth to make a difference through school assembly presentations, workshops, and summer camps.

> *"I learned more about what really matters to me in one hour with YES! than I did in all of 9th grade."*
>
> Amy Holstine, Centerville, Ohio

YES! CAMPS

Are you a young person who wants to make our world a better place? Do you want to meet other youth who share your concern and your desire to act? Hundreds of people have come to YES! Camps and left saying it was one of the most important experiences of their lives. Come see what they're talking about. Experience the growth, fun, and magic.

> *"Inspiring, touching, refreshing. It challenged me to be real and to look for the truth in myself and those around me."*
>
> Melissa Farrow, Los Angeles, Calif.

STUDENT ACTION GUIDE

Through years of experience working with hundreds of environmental groups, we've learned a great deal about what makes some groups work and others fail. The YES! *Student Action Guide* provides ideas and resources for maintaining a successful organization or school club, running meetings, and raising funds. Available from YES! for $5, including postage and handling.

"JUST THE FACTS"

"Earth Action Guide" is a booklet of facts excerpted from *Choices for Our Future*. Available from YES! for $3, including postage and handling.

HOW TO GET INVOLVED

To find out about YES!, sending a contribution, coming to a summer camp, being part of the Green Schools Program, or to get a fact booklet or Youth Action Guide, contact:

YES!
706 Frederick St.
Santa Cruz, CA 95062
(408) 459-9344

RESOURCES

WORKING FOR POSITIVE CHANGE

- ◆Action for Corporate Accountability, 129 Church St., New Haven, CT 06510 (203) 787-0061

- ◆Amnesty International USA, 322 Eighth Ave., New York, NY 10001 (212) 807-8400

- ◆Beyond Beef, 1130 17th St., NW, Suite 300, Washington, D.C. 20036 (202) 775-1132

- ◆Cultural Survival, 215 First St., Cambridge, MA 02142 (617) 621-3818

- ◆Earth Force, 1501 Wilson Blvd., 12th Fl., Arlington, VA 22209

- ◆Earth Island Institute, 300 Broadway, Suite 28, San Francisco, CA 94133 (415) 788-3666

- ◆Earth Train, P.O. Box 1668, Orinda, CA 94563 (510) 254-9101

- ◆EarthSave, 706 Frederick St., Santa Cruz, CA 95062 (408) 423-4069

- ◆Environmental Youth Alliance, P.O. Box 34097, Station D, Vancouver, BC, Canada V6J 4MI (604) 737-2258

- ◆Friends Of The Earth, 218 D St., SE, Washington, D.C. 20003 (202) 544-2600

- ◆Greenhouse Crisis Foundation, 1130 17th St., NW, Suite 630, Washington, D.C. 20036 (202) 466-2823

- ◆Greenpeace USA, 1436 "U" Street, NW, Washington, D.C. 20009 (202) 462-1177

- Indigenous Environmental Network, Youth Task Force, P.O. Box 1253, Farmington, NM 87401

- Kids Against Pollution, 275 High St., Closter, NJ 07624 (201) 768-1332

- Kids For A Clean Environment (Kids FACE), P.O. Box 158254, Nashville, TN 37215

- National Association for the Advancement of Colored People (NAACP), 4805 Mt. Hope Dr., Baltimore, MD 21215 (410) 358-8900

- National Audubon Society, 645 Pennsylvania Ave., SE, Washington, D.C. 20003

- National Wildlife Federation, 1400 16th St., NW, Washington, D.C. 20036

- Natural Resources Defense Council, 40 W. 20th St., New York, NY 10011

- Ozone Action, 34 Wall St., Suite 203, Asheville, NC 28801 (704) 254-3811

- People for the Ethical Treatment of Animals, P.O. Box 42516, Washington, D.C. 20015 (202) 770-7444

- The Rainbow Coalition, P.O. Box 27385, Washington, D.C. 20036 (202) 728-1180

- Rainforest Action Network, 450 Sansome, Suite 700 San Francisco, CA 94111 (415) 398-4404

- Save America's Forests, 4 Library Court, SE, Washington, D.C. 20003 (202) 544-9219

- Sierra Club, 730 Polk St., San Francisco, CA 94109 (415) 776-2211

- Sierra Student Coalition, 223 Thayer St., # 2, Providence, RI 02906 (401) 861-6012

- Student Environmental Action Coalition, P.O. Box 1168, Chapel Hill, NC 27514 (919) 967-4600

- United Farm Workers, P.O. Box 62, La Paz Street Keane, CA 93531 (805) 822-5571

◆ Unplug Channel One, 360 Grand Ave., Box 385,
Oakland, CA 94610 (510) 268-1100

◆ Youth for Environmental Sanity (YES!), 706 Frederick
St., Santa Cruz, CA 95062 (408) 459-9344

◆ Zero Population Growth, 1400 10th St., NW, Suite 320,
Washington, D.C. 20036

USEFUL RESOURCES

◆ To get your name off junk mail lists, contact:
Mail Preference Service, ℅ Direct Marketing Assn., 11
W. 42nd St., New York, NY 10163

◆ To locate the food bank nearest you, call or write:
Second Harvest, 116 South Michigan Avenue
Suite 4, Chicago, IL 60603 (312) 263-2303

◆ For the name and address of your closest food co-op,
contact: The National Cooperative Business Institute,
1401 New York Avenue, N.W., Suite 1100
Washington, DC 20005 (202) 638-6222

◆ To find out about adopting acres of rainforest, write to:
Protect-an-Acre Program, Rainforest Action Network,
450 Sansome, Suite 700, San Francisco, CA 94111
(415)398-4404

◆ For more information on local diaper services, contact:
The National Association of Diaper Services, 2017
Walnut St., Philadelphia, PA 19103 (215) 569-3650

◆ To order a copy of *Students Shopping for a Better
World*, contact: Council On Economic Priorities, (800)-
729-4237. Or write CEP, 30 Irving Place, New York,
NY, 10003. The price is $6 from bookstores, or $7.50
with postage and handling through the mail.

♦ Organic Food Mail Order Supplies from Americans For Safe Food, 1501 16th St., N.W., Washington, DC 20036 (202) 332-9110. This listing will help you find mail-order sources for garlic, olive oil, walnuts, almonds, pecans, kiwi fruit, sun dried tomatoes, potato chips and much more—all completely organic.

♦ For information on organic gardening and how to do it, contact Rodale Press, 33 East Minor Street, Emmaus, PA 18098; (215) 967-5171. They publish *Organic Gardening* magazine, and numerous books on the subject.

CATALOGS OF ENVIRONMENTALLY SENSITIVE PRODUCTS

♦ Eco-Source Catalogue, 380 South Morris St. Sebastopol, CA 95472 (800) 688-8345

♦ Real Goods Trading Corporation, 966 Mazzoni St. Ukiah, CA, 95482-3471 (800) 762-7325

♦ Real Recycled, 1541 Adrian Rd., Burlingame, CA 94010-2107 (800) 233-5335

♦ Seventh Generation, 49 Hercules Dr., Colchester, VT 05446-1177 (800) 456-1177

RECOMMENDED BOOKS

♦ *Alternatives To The Peace Corps,* edited by Becky Buell, Victoria Clark, and Susan Leone, Food First Books, San Francisco, Calif, 1992

♦ *Backyard Composting,* written and published by Harmonious Technologies, Ojai, Calif, 1992. To order, contact: Publishers' Distribution Service, 6893 Sullivan Rd., Grawn, MI 49637 or (if you have Visa or Master-Card) call (800) 345-0096.

- *Beyond Beef,* by Jeremy Rifkin, Dutton, New York, N.Y., 1992
- *Climate In Crisis,* by Albert Bates, The Book Publishing Company, Summertown, Tenn., 1990
- *Diet for a New America,* by John Robbins, Stillpoint Publishing, Walpole, N.H., 1987
- *Earth In The Balance,* by Vice President Albert Gore, Houghton Mifflin Co., Boston, Mass., 1992
- *The Ecology Of Commerce,* by Paul Hawken, HarperCollins Publishers, New York, N.Y., 1993
- *The Emperor Wears No Clothes,* by Jack Herer, HEMP Publishing, Van Nuys, Calif., 1990
- *Four Arguments For The Elimination Of Television,* by Jerry Mander, Quill Publishing, New York, N.Y., 1978
- *Fundraising For Social Change,* by Kim Klein, Chardon Press, Inverness, Calif., 1988
- *Gaia: An Atlas Of Planet Management,* by Norman Myers, Anchor Press/Doubleday, New York, NY, 1984
- *The Green Consumer,* by John Elkington, Julia Hailes and Joel Makower, Penguin Books, New York, N.Y., 1990
- *How To Make The World A Better Place,* by Jeffrey Hollender, William Morrow & Company Inc. New York, N.Y., 1990
- *If You Love This Planet,* by Helen Caldicott, MD, W.W. Norton & Co., New York, N.Y., 1992
- *In The Absence Of The Sacred: The failure of technology and the survival of the Indian nations* by Jerry Mander, Sierra Club Books San Francisco, Calif., 1991

- *May All Be Fed,* by John Robbins, William Morrow & Company Inc., New York, N.Y., 1990

- *The New Farm Vegetarian Cookbook,* edited by Louise Hagler and Dorothy Bates, The Book Publishing Company, Summertown, Tenn., 1988

- *The Rainforest Book,* by Scott Lewis and the Natural Resources Defense Council, Berkeley Books New York, N.Y., 1990

- *State Of The World,* by Worldwatch, W.W. Norton & Co., New York, N.Y., updated annually

- *Students Shopping for a Better World*, written and published by Council On Economic Priorities, New York, N.Y., 1992

- *Thinking Like A Mountain,* by John Seed, Joanna Macy, and Bill Devall, New Society Publishers Santa Cruz, Calif., 1988

- *The Population Explosion,* by Paul Ehrlich and Anne Ehrlich, Touchstone / Simon & Schuster, New York, N.Y., 1990

- *When Technology Wounds,* by Chellis Glendinning, William Morrow & Company Inc., New York, N.Y., 1990

RECOMMENDED MAGAZINES

- *Adbusters*, 1243 West 7th Avenue, Vancouver, BC, Canada V6H 1B7 (604) 736-9401

- *Boycott News*, published by Institute for Consumer Responsibility, 6506 28th Ave., NE, Seattle, WA 98115 (206) 523-0421

- *E: The Environmental Magazine*, P.O. Box 6667, Syracuse, NY 13217-7934 (800) 825-0061

- *Earth First! Journal*, P.O. Box 5871, Tucson, AZ 85703 (602) 622-1371

- *Earth Island Journal*, 300 Broadway, Suite 28, San Francisco, CA 94133-3312 (415) 788-3666

- *Multinational Monitor*, P.O. Box 19405, Washington, DC 20036 (202) 387-8030

- *The Utne Reader*, P.O. Box 1974, Marion, OH 43306-2074 (800) 736-UTNE

- *Worldwatch*, 1776 Massachusetts Ave., NW, Washington, D.C. 20036 (202) 452-1999

WRITE LETTERS EXPRESSING YOUR FEELINGS, THOUGHTS AND CONCERNS TO:

- Edgar Woolard, Jr., Chairman of the Board, Du Pont Corporation, 1007 Market Street, Wilmington, DE 19898. Or call Du Pont at: (800) 441-7515.

- Lewis Preston, President, The World Bank, 1818 "H" Street, NW, Washington, D.C. 20433

- Mr. Shimoroku Morahashi, Mitsubishi Corporation, 263 Marunouchi, Chiyoda-ku, Tokyo, Japan

- Tim Crull, President, Nestlé USA, 800 North Brand Blvd., Glendale, CA 91203

- John Stafford, President, American Home Products 685 Third Avenue, New York, NY 10017

YOUR ELECTED REPRESENTATIVES

♦ *The President of The United States*, The White House, 1600 Pennsylvania Ave., NW, Washington, DC 20500

♦ *Your Senator*, U.S. Senate, Washington, DC 20510

♦ *Your Congressional Representative*, U.S. House of Representatives, Washington, D.C. 20515

To find out who your elected representatives are, look up the "Government Offices" or the "Federal Government" section of your local phone book.

RECYCLING INFORMATION

Contact your state's solid waste office to find out what can be recycled, and where, in your region. This list was updated by the EPA in 1992, so it's possible some of these numbers have changed.

Alabama	Alaska	Arizona	Arkansas
(205) 271-7726	(907) 465-5150	(602) 207-4121	(501) 562-7444
California	Colorado	Connecticut	Delaware
(916) 255-2182	(303) 331-4822	(203) 566-8844	(302) 739-3829
Florida	Georgia	Hawaii	Idaho
(904) 922-6104	(404) 362-2695	(808) 586-4240	(208) 334-5898
Illinois	Indiana	Iowa	Kansas
(217) 785-8604	(317) 232-3501	(515) 281-6284	(913) 296-1594
Kentucky	Louisiana	Maine	Maryland
(502) 564-6716	(504) 342-1216	(207) 289-2651	(410) 631-3364

Massachusetts (617) 292-5961	Michigan (517) 373-9523	Minnesota (612) 296-7340	Mississippi (601) 961-5047
Missouri (314) 751-5401	Montana (406) 444-1430	Nebraska (402) 471-2186	Nevada (702) 687-5872
New Hampshire (603) 271-3505	New Jersey (609) 530-8591	New Mexico (505) 827-2959	New York (518) 457-6603
North Carolina (919) 733-0692	North Dakota (701) 221-5166	Ohio (614) 644-3181	Oklahoma (405) 271-7159
Oregon (503) 229-5356	Pennsylvania (717) 783-2388	Rhode Island (401) 277-2787	South Carolina (803) 734-5200
South Dakota (605) 773-4222	Tennessee (615) 741-3424	Texas (512) 458-7271	Utah (801) 538-6170
Vermont (802) 244-7831	Virginia (804) 225-2667	Washington (206 459-6316	Washington, D.C. (202) 939-8115
West Virginia (304) 348-5929	Wisconsin (608)266-0520	Wyoming (307) 777-7752	

ENDNOTES

CHAPTER TWO
LIFE ON EARTH

1. The World Wildlife Fund, *Atlas of The Environment,* Prentice Hall Press, 1990, p. 89.

2. Paulette Bauer Middleton, 1992 *Earth Journal,* "Pollution," Buzzworm Books, 1992, p. 81.

3. The World Wildlife Fund, *Atlas of The Environment,* Prentice Hall Press, 1990, p. 92.

4. The World Wildlife Fund, *Atlas of The Environment,* Prentice Hall Press, 1990, p. 92.

5. Hillary French et al, The Worldwatch Institute, *State of The World 1990,* W.W. Norton & Co., 1990, p. 98.

6. Hillary French, *Worldwatch Magazine,* May/June, 1990, p. 27.

7. Hillary French et al, The Worldwatch Institute, *State of The World 1990,* W.W. Norton & Co., 1990, p. 104.

8. Jeffrey Hollender, *How To Make The World A Better Place,* William Morrow & Co., Inc., 1990, p. 49.

9. Mary Metzger and Cynthia P. Whittaker, *This Planet Is Mine,* Simon & Schuster, 1991, p. 41.

10. *Water Treatment Handbook,* Northeast Publishing, pp. 9-13.

11. Chellis Glendinning, *When Technology Wounds,* William Morrow & Co., Inc., 1990, p. 77.

12. Jacqueline MacDonald, *Garbage,* March/April, 1991, p. 32.

13. Lawrence Tasaday, *Shopping For A Better Environment,* Meadowbrook Press, 1991, p. 170.

14. John Elkington, Julia Hailes, and Joel Makower, *The Green Consumer,* Penguin Books, 1988, p. 128.

15. Albert K. Bates, *Climate in Crisis,* Book Publishing Company, 1990, p. 18.

16. Jeremy Rifkin and Carol Grunewald Rifkin, *Voting Green,* Doubleday, 1992, p. 189

17. David Fishman, *E: The Environmental Magazine*, January/February, 1990, p. 36.

CHAPTER THREE
TURNING THE EARTH INTO PRODUCTS

18. Allan Durning, *Worldwatch*, November/December, 1990, p. 12.

19. Kono Matsu, *Adbusters*, Winter, 1993, p. 56.

20. Kono Matsu, *Adbusters*, Winter, 1993, p. 56.

21. Council on Economic Priorities, *Students Shopping For A Better World*, 1993, p. 25.

22. Kalle Lasn, Cat Simril, and Barbara Green, *Adbusters*, vol. 1, no. 3, p. 9.

23. Donella Meadows, *Anals of Earth*, vol. 7, no.1, 1989, p. 10.

24. Concern, Inc., *Waste: Choices for Communities*, Washington, D.C., p. 5.

25. Chellis Glendinning, *When Technology Wounds*, William Morrow & Company, 1990, p. 98.

26. John Young, *Worldwatch Magazine*, July-August, 1991, p. 8.

27. Bill Breen, *Garbage Magazine*, March/April, 1991, p. 45.

28. Barry Commoner, *The New York Times*, January 29, 1989.

29. Bill Breen, *Garbage Magazine*, March/April, 1991, p. 48.

30. Judy Christrup, *Greenpeace Magazine*, May/June, 1988, p. 11.

31. Bill Breen, *Garbage Magazine*, March/April, 1991, p. 47

32. Susan Hassol and Beth Richman, *Recycling*, A Windstar EarthPulse Handbook, 1989, p. 19.

33. Susan Hassol and Beth Richman, *Recycling*, A Windstar EarthPulse Handbook, 1989, p. 19.

34. Bill Breen, *Garbage Magazine*, March/April, 1991, p. 45.

35. Prepared by Cerrel Associates of Los Angeles, Calif., for the California Waste Management Board, as quoted in *No Time To Waste*, a video produced by Greenpeace.

36. Derived from Robert Bullard, *Multinational Monitor*, June, 1992, p. 22.

37. Judy Christrup, *Greenpeace Magazine*, May/June, 1988, p. 10.

38. Bill Breen, *Garbage Magazine*, March/April, 1991, p. 49.

39. Bill Breen, *Garbage Magazine*, March/April, 1991, p. 49.

40. Bill Breen, *Garbage Magazine*, March/April, 1991, p. 49.

41. Judy Christrup, *Greenpeace Magazine*, May/June, 1988, p. 11.

42. Judy Christrup, *Greenpeace Magazine*, May/June, 1988, p. 11.

CHAPTER FOUR
CHOOSING TO CUT THE TRASH

43. Susan Hassol and Beth Richman, *Recycling*, A Windstar Earth-Pulse Handbook, 1989, p. 25.

44. The Earth Works Group, *50 Simple Things You Can Do To Save The Earth*, Earth Works Press, 1989, p. 68.

45. King County Nurses Association, Seattle, Wash., *Hazards Posed By The Improper Disposal Of Disposable Diapers* fact sheet.

46. *Waste: Choices for Communities*, Concern, Inc., Washington, D.C., p. 13.

47. John Robbins, *May All Be Fed*, William Morrow & Co., Inc., 1992, p. 172.

48. William Chandler, *State Of The World 1984*, W.W. Norton & Co., 1984, p. 95.

49. The Earth Works Group, *50 Simple Things You Can Do To Save The Earth*, Earth Works Press, 1989, p. 64.

50. The Earth Works Group, *50 Simple Things You Can Do To Save The Earth*, Earth Works Press, 1989, p. 64.

51. Environmental Defense Fund brochure *"If You're Not Recycling, You're Throwing It All Away,"* 1988.

52. The Earth Works Group, *50 Simple Things You Can Do To Save The Earth*, Earth Works Press, 1989, p. 62.

53. Environmental Action Foundation, Washington, D.C., Solid Waste Fact Packet.

54. The Earth Works Group, *50 Simple Things You Can Do To Save The Earth*, Earth Works Press, 1989, p. 72.

55. Susan Hassol and Beth Richman, *Recycling*, A Windstar EarthPulse Handbook, 1989, p. 60.

56. Debra Lynn Dadd and Andre Carothers, *Greenpeace*, May/June, 1990, p. 11.

57. *EcoCycle Times,* vol. 12, no. 1, Boulder, Colo., p. 7.

58. *EcoCycle Times,* vol. 12, no. 1, Boulder, Colo., p. 7.

59. *Backyard Composting,* Harmonious Press, 1992, p. 7.

60. *Backyard Composting,* Harmonious Press, 1992, p. 75.

61. *Backyard Composting,* Harmonious Press, 1992, p. 7.

62. Institute of Scrap Recycling Industries, Washington, D.C., p. 6, p. 12.

63. *Prescott Peace News,* Prescott, Ariz., January, 1989, p. 9.

64. *The Greenpeace Guide To Paper,* 1990, p. 40.

65. Ed Ayres, *Worldwatch,* September/October, 1992, p. 21.

66. Ed Ayres, *Worldwatch,* September/October, 1992, p. 18.

Chapter Five
Power to the Buyer

67. I. Wallace et. al., adapted from *Book of Lists #2,* Bantam Books, 1980, p. 107.

68. Todd Putnam, *National Boycott News,* Winter 1992-93, p. 25.

69. John Robbins, *Diet for a New America,* Stillpoint, 1987, p. 39.

70. John Robbins, *Diet for a New America,* Stillpoint, 1987, p. 39.

71. As quoted in the documentary video, *Deadly Deception*, produced by INFACT.

72. Chellis Glendinning, *When Technology Wounds,* William Morrow & Company, Inc., 1990, p. 43.

73. Michael Renner et. al., Worldwatch, State *of the World 1991,* W.W. Norton & Company, 1991, p. 145.

74. *Deadly Deception*, a documentary video produced by INFACT.

75. *Deadly Deception*, a documentary video produced by INFACT.

76. *Deadly Deception*, a documentary video produced by INFACT.

77. *Deadly Deception*, a documentary video produced by INFACT.

78. *Nuclear Weaponmakers Campaign Update,* a publication of INFACT, Winter, 1993.

79. *Deadly Deception*, a documentary video produced by INFACT.

80. United Nations Environment Program, *Executive Summary, Environmental Effects of Ozone Depletion;* November, 1991.

81. NASA/NOAA Press Brief, Washington, D.C., October 16, 1993.

82. *Toronto Globe and Mail,* Wednesday, February 12, 1992.

83. *Ozone Action Reports,* produced by Ozone Action, Asheville, N.C.

84. *Ozone Action Reports,* produced by Ozone Action, Asheville, N.C.

85. Todd Putnam, *National Boycott News,* Winter 1992-93, p. 80.

86. Todd Putnam, *National Boycott News,* Winter 1992-93, p. 82.

87. Andre Carothers, *Greenpeace* magazine, July/August, 1990, p. 11.

88. Danny Duncan, *The Wheatsville Breeze,* June, 1991, p. 4.

89. Action for Corporate Accountability, *Action Update,* Fall, 1991, p. 1.

90. John Robbins, *May All Be Fed,* William Morrow & Co., Inc., 1992, p. 129.

91. Action for Corporate Accountability, *Action Update,* Fall, 1991, p. 1.

92. Christopher Plant with David H. Albert, *Green Business: Hope Or Hoax?,* New Society Publishers, 1991, p. 4.

93. Justin Lowe and Hillary Hansen, *Earth Island Journal,* Winter, 1990, p. 26.

94. Justin Lowe and Hillary Hansen, *Earth Island Journal,* Winter, 1990, p. 27.

95. Justin Lowe and Hillary Hansen, *Earth Island Journal,* Winter, 1990, p. 27.

96. Justin Lowe and Hillary Hansen, *Earth Island Journal,* Winter, 1990, p. 27.

97. Justin Lowe and Hillary Hansen, *Earth Island Journal,* Winter, 1990, p. 27.

98. Justin Lowe and Hillary Hansen, *Earth Island Journal,* Winter, 1990, p. 27.

CHAPTER SIX
CHOW NO COW

99. Lester Brown et. al., Worldwatch, *State of the World 1992,* W.W. Norton & Company, 1992, p. 3.

100. Lester Brown et al, Worldwatch, *State of the World 1992,* W.W. Norton & Company, 1990, pp. 4-5.

101. Lester Brown et al, Worldwatch, *State of the World 1992,* W.W. Norton & Company, 1990, pp. 4-5.

102. Worldwatch Paper no. 62, *Management In An Age Of Scarcity,* 1984, p. 25.

103. Seth King, *The New York Times,* December 5, 1976, p. 61.

104. Lester Brown et al, Worldwatch, *State of the World 1992,* W.W. Norton & Comany, 1990, pp. 3-4.

105. John Robbins, *Diet for a New America,* Stillpoint, 1987, p. 352.

106. John Robbins, *Diet for a New America,* Stillpoint, 1987, p. 352.

107. Mary Bralove, *The Wall Street Journal,* October 3, 1974, p. 20.

108. John Robbins, *Diet for a New America,* Stillpoint, 1987, p. 351.

109. H.J. Maidenburg, *The New York Times,* July 1, 1973, p. 1.

110. U.S. Department of Agriculture, Economic Research Service, Beltsville, Md., as cited in Frances Moore Lappé, *Diet for a Small Planet,* tenth anniversary edition, 1982, p. 70.

111. U.S. Department of Agriculture, Economic Research Service, Beltsville, Md., as cited in Frances Moore Lappé, *Diet for a Small Planet,* tenth anniversary edition, 1982, p. 70.

112. Harvey Diamond, *Your Heart, Your Planet,* Hay House, 1990, pp. 60-61.

113. Harvey Diamond, *Your Heart, Your Planet,* Hay House, 1990, p. 61.

114. Tom Aldridge and Herb Schlubach, *Soil and Water,* University of California Cooperative Extension, Fall 1978, no. 38, pp. 13-17.

115. Statistical Abstract of the United States Department of Agriculture (USDA), Chart no. 1148, 1982-1983.

116. John Robbins, *May All Be Fed,* William Morrow & Company, 1992, on cover.

117. John Robbins, *May All Be Fed,* William Morrow & Company, 1992, p. 40.

118. Boyce Resenberger, *The New York Times,* October 25, 1974.

119. John Robbins, *Diet for a New America,* Stillpoint, 1987, pp. 371-373.

120. John Robbins, *Diet for a New America,* Stillpoint, 1987, p. 372.

121. William Lagrone, Shertz et. al., USDA, ESCS, *The Great Plains,* Agricultural Economic Report no. 441, December, 1979.

122. John Robbins, *Diet for a New America,* Stillpoint, 1987, p. 371.

123. Frances Moore Lappé, *Diet for a Small Planet,* Tenth Anniversary Edition, Ballantine Books, 1982, p. 69.

124. Georg Borgrstrom, at the annual meeting of the American Association for the Advancement of Science, 1981.

125. Dr. David Fields and Robin Hur, *Vegetarian Times,* February, 1984.

126. William F. Allman, *US News & World Report,* October 31, 1988, p. 68.

127. Allan Durning & Worldwatch, *How Much Is Enough,* W.W. Norton & Co., Inc., 1992, p. 68.

128. John Robbins, *Animals' Voice Magazine,* February, 1989, p. 6.

129. W. Kannel, *New England Journal of Medicine,* 311:1144, 1984.

130. C. Walles, *Time Magazine,* March 26, 1984, p. 62.

131. C. Walles, *Time Magazine,* March 26, 1984, p. 62.

132. USDA Agriculture Handbook No. 456.

133. John McDougall, M.D., *McDougall's Medicine: A Challenging Second Opinion,* New Win Publishing, 1985, p. 75.

134. Jeffrey Hollender, *How To Make The World A Better Place,* William Morrow & Co., Inc., 1990, p. 121.

135. John Robbins, *Diet for a New America,* Stillpoint, 1987, pp. 48-145 (discussing chickens, pigs, and cows).

136. John Robbins, *Diet for a New America,* Stillpoint, 1987, pp. 48-145 (discussing chickens, pigs, and cows).

137. John Robbins, *Diet for a New America,* Stillpoint, 1987, pp. 48-145 (discussing chickens, pigs, and cows).

CHAPTER SEVEN
EATING FOR A HEALTHY WORLD

138. John Elkington, Julia Hailes, and Joel Makower, *The Green Consumer*, Penguin Books, 1990, p. 82.

139. Chellis Glendinning, *When Technology Wounds,* William Morrow & Co., Inc., 1990, p. 56.

140. Chellis Glendinning, *When Technology Wounds,* William Morrow & Co., Inc., 1990, p. 56.

141. John Elkington, Julia Hailes, and Joel Makower, *The Green Consumer*, Penguin Books, 1990, p. 83.

142. Chellis Glendinning, *When Technology Wounds,* William Morrow & Co., Inc., 1990, p. 55.

143. Jeffrey Hollender, *How To Make The World A Better Place,* William Morrow & Co., Inc., 1990, p. 129.

144. Reynolds Holding, *The San Francisco Chronicle,* March 2, 1993.

145. John Elkington, Julia Hailes, and Joel Makower, *The Green Consumer*, Penguin Books,, 1990, p. 84.

146. Robert Wasserstrom and Richard Wiles, *Field Duty: U.S. Farm workers and Pesticide Safety,* Study 3 (World Resources Institute, Washington, D.C.), 1985, p. 2.

147. Jeffrey Hollender, *How To Make The World A Better Place,* William Morrow & Co., Inc., 1990, pp. 129-130.

148. Allan Durning & Worldwatch, *How Much Is Enough,* W.W. Norton & Co., Inc., 1992, p. 73.

149. Jeffrey Hollender, *How To Make The World A Better Place,* William Morrow & Co., Inc., 1990, p. 131.

150. Jeffrey Hollender, *How To Make The World A Better Place,* William Morrow & Co., Inc., 1990, p. 133.

151. Jeffrey Hollender, *How To Make The World A Better Place,* William Morrow & Co., Inc., 1990, p. 134.

152. Jeffrey Hollender, *How To Make The World A Better Place,* William Morrow & Co., Inc., 1990, p. 134.

CHAPTER EIGHT
ENERGY CHOICES

153. Energy Information Administration's *Monthly Energy Review,* December, 1988, p. 15.

154. Susan Hassol and Beth Richman, *Energy,* A Windstar EarthPulse Handbook, 1989, p. 16.

155. *Scholastic Update,* April 19, 1991, p. 5.

156. Carrying Capacity, Inc., *Beyond Oil—A Summary Report,* Ballinger Publishing Co., 1986, p. 7.

157. Mike Leary, *The Philadelphia Inquirer,* October 4, 1987.

158. Hillary French et al, Worldwatch Institute, *State of the World 1990,* W.W. Norton, 1990, p. 107.

159. John Elkington, Julia Hailes, and Joel Makower, *The Green Consumer,* Penguin Books, 1990, p. 13.

160. John Elkington, Julia Hailes, and Joel Makower, *The Green Consumer,* Penguin Books, 1990, p. 13.

161. John Elkington, Julia Hailes, and Joel Makower, *The Green Consumer,* Penguin Books, 1990, p. 13.

162. John Elkington, Julia Hailes, and Joel Makower, *The Green Consumer,* Penguin Books, 1990, p. 14.

163. Albert K. Bates, *Climate in Crisis,* Book Publishing Company, 1990, p. 10.

164. William F. Allman, *US News & World Report,* October 31, 1988, p. 60.

165. World Wildlife Fund, *Atlas of the Environment,* Prentice Hall Press, 1990, p. 93.

166. Michael Parish, *Los Angeles Times,* August 15, 1989.

167. Ramanathan, *Journal of Geophysical Research,* 1985, pp. 5547-66.

168. Albert K. Bates, *Climate in Crisis,* Book Publishing Company, 1990, p. 46.

169. William F. Allman, *US News & World Report,* October 31, 1988, p. 61.

170. Lester R. Brown, *Worldwatch Paper 85,* October, 1988, p. 39.

171. World Wildlife Fund, *Atlas of the Environment,* Prentice Hall Press, 1990, p. 176.

172. World Wildlife Fund, *Atlas of the Environment,* Prentice Hall Press, 1990, p. 176.

173. The Earth Works Group, *30 Simple Energy Things You Can Do To Save The Earth,* Earth Works Press, 1990, p. 59.

174. From The Editors Of Buzzworm Magazine, *1992 Earth Journal,* Buzzworm Books, 1992, p. 263.

175. The Union of Concerned Scientists, *Steering A New Course,* 1991, p. 47.

176. The Union of Concerned Scientists, *Steering A New Course,* 1991, p. 47.

177. The Alliance for a Paving Moratorium, *The Problem With Paving,* Fact Sheet no. 1.

178. The Worldwatch Institute, *State of the World 1989,* Michael Renner, et. al., W.W. Norton & Co., 1989, p. 112.

179. *Issues Review and Tracking: The Energy Newsbrief,* vol. 4, no. 1, January 5, 1989.

180. The Earth Works Group, *50 Simple Things You Can Do To Save The Earth,* Earth Works Press, 1990, p. 89.

181. The Union of Concerned Scientists, *Steering A New Course,* 1991, p. 124.

182. The Alliance for a Paving Moratorium, *The Problem With Paving,* Fact Sheet #1.

183. United States Energy Administration Annual Energy Review, 1990.

184. The Union of Concerned Scientists, *Nucleus Quarterly,* vol. 12, no. 3, Fall, 1990, p. 1.

185. J. Baldwin, *Whole Earth Review,* No. 68, Fall 1990, pp. 32-33.

186. John Robbins, *The War, Oil And Your Dinner,* unpublished, 1991.

187. extrapolated from *Household Vehicles Energy Consumption, 1988,* Department of Energy-Energy Information Administration, 0464, 1988.

188. Rick Bevington and Arthur Rosenfeld, *Scientific American,* vol. 263, no. 3, September, 1990, p. 77.

189. Jeff Peline, *The San Francisco Chronicle,* unknown date, Fall 1993, p. D1.

190. Michael Klaper, M.D., *Fuel For The Future,* unpublished, 1991.

191. Jay Stein, *The Amicus Journal,* Spring 1990, p. 33.

192. Jay Stein, *The Amicus Journal,* Spring 1990, p. 36.

193. Arnold Ficket et al, *Scientific American,* vol. 263, no. 3, September 1990, p. 74.

194. Arnold Ficket et al, *Scientific American,* vol. 263, no. 3, September 1990, p. 74.

195. H. Akbari, et. al., *The Impact Of Summer Heat Islands On Cooling Energy Consumption And CO2 Emissions,* Lawrence Berkeley Laboratory, University of California, July 1988, p. 8.

196. The Earth Works Group, *30 Simple Energy Things You Can Do To Save The Earth,* Earth Works Press, 1990, p. 22.

197. Kirk B. Smith, *The Green Lifestyle Handbook,* Henry Holt & Company, 1990, p. 4.

198. The Earth Works Group, *50 Simple Things You Can Do To Save The Earth,* Earth Works Press, 1990, p. 54.

199. The Earth Works Group, *50 Simple Things You Can Do To Save The Earth,* Earth Works Press, 1990, p. 54.

200. Arnold Ficket, et. al., *Scientific American,* vol. 263, no. 3, September 1990, p. 68.

201. Rick Bevington and Arthur Rosenfeld, *Scientific American,* vol. 263, no. 3, September 1990, p. 82.

CHAPTER NINE
ENERGY AND THE FUTURE OF LIFE

202. Christopher Flavin and Nicholas Lenssen, *Worldwatch*, September/October 1991, p. 11.

203. Public Citizen, as quoted in *Earth Island Journal,* Summer 1989, p. 28.

204. Christopher Flavin and Nicholas Lenssen, *Worldwatch*, September/October 1991, p. 12.

205. Christopher Flavin ad Nicholas Lenssen, *Worldwatch*, September/October 1991, p. 12.

206. Louis Peck, *Garbage*, January/February, 1991, p. 28.

207. Christopher Flavin and Nicholas Lenssen, *Worldwatch*, September/October 1991, p. 13

208. Christopher Flavin and Nicholas Lenssen, *Worldwatch*, September/October 1991, p. 13

209. Alan Miller, Irving Mintzer and Sara Hoagland, *Growing Power,* The World Resources Institute Study 5, April 1986, p. 6.

210. Jack Herer, *Earth Island Journal,* Fall 1990, p. 36.

211. Paul Stanford, as quoted in *The Oregonian,* January 22, 1990.

212. W. DaSilva, Sunday *Punch,* Sydney, Australia, March 24, 1991.

213. Alan W. Bock, (senior columnist) *The Orange County Register,* May 3, 1990.

214. Brent Moore, *The Hemp Industry In Kentucky: A Study Of The Past, The Present, And The Possibilities,* James E. Hughes Press, 1905, pp. 69-71.

215. Tracey Jefferys-Renault, *The Epicenter,* June 14, 1990, p. 6.

216. Allan Teramuara, University of Maryland study, *Discover*, September, 1989.

217. Jim Cavendar, Ohio University Botany Professor, as quoted in *Athens News,* article by Jim Phillips, vol. 13: 92, November 16, 1989.

218. L.H. Dewey, *United States Department of Agriculture Yearbook,* 1913, U.S. GPO. Washington, D.C., 1914, pp. 305-326.

219. Brent Moore, *The Hemp Industry In Kentucky: A Study Of The Past, The Present, And The Possibilities,* James E. Hughes Press, 1905, p. 111.

220. *Science News Letter,* September 8, 1945, p. 158.

221. Levi-Strauss & Company of San Francisco, Calif., personal communication with Gene McClaine, 1985.

222. Ernest Ebel, from the diaries of George Washington and Thomas Jefferson, as printed in *Marijuana: The First 12,000 Years,* Plenum Press, 1980.

223. V.S. Clark, *History of Manufacture in the United States,* McGraw Hill, N.Y., 1929, p. 34.

224. Jack Herer, *Earth Island Journal,* Fall 1990, p. 37.

225. Jack Herer, *The Emperor Wears No Clothes,* Queen Of Clubs, 1990, p. 23.

226. Dr. Lester Grinspoon, *Scientific American,* vol. 221:6, December, 1969.

227. Marion Furr & Paul G. Mahlberg, *Journal of Natural Products,* vol. 44:2, March, 1981, pp. 153-159.

228. Paul Ehrlich and Anne Ehrlich, *The Population Bomb,* Simon & Schuster, Inc., 1990, p. 14.

229. Paul Ehrlich and Anne Ehrlich, *The Population Bomb,* Simon & Schuster, Inc., 1990, p. 14.

230. World Wildlife Fund, *Atlas of the Environment,* Prentice Hall Press, 1990, p. 19.

231. World Information Transfer, *The WIT Report,* vol. III, no. 3, May/June 1991, p. 7.

232. World Wildlife Fund, *Atlas of the Environment,* Prentice Hall Press, 1990, p. 19.

233. Leslie Pardue, *E Magazine,* November/December, 1990, p. 47.

234. World Wildlife Fund, *Atlas of the Environment,* Prentice Hall Press, 1990, p. 20.

CHAPTER TEN
THE TROPICAL RAINFORESTS

235. The World Wildlife Fund, *Atlas of The Environment,* Prentice Hall Press, 1990, pp. 65-68.

236. John Robbins, *Diet for a New America,* Stillpoint, 1987, p. 363.

237. Scott Lewis, *The Rainforest Book,* Living Planet Press, 1990, p. 15.

238. Scott Lewis, *The Rainforest Book,* Living Planet Press, 1990, p. 15.

239. Scott Lewis, *The Rainforest Book,* Living Planet Press, 1990, p. 27.

240. Scott Lewis, *The Rainforest Book,* Living Planet Press, 1990, p. 27.

241. John Elkington, Julia Hailes, and Joel Makower, *The Green Consumer,* Penguin Books, 1988, p. 25.

242. John Robbins, *Diet for a New America,* Stillpoint, 1987, p. 365.

243. The World Wildlife Fund, *Atlas of The Environment,* Prentice Hall Press, 1990, pp. 65-68.

244. John Elkington, Julia Hailes, and Joel Makower, *The Green Consumer,* Penguin Books, 1988, p. 24.

245. Scott Lewis, *The Rainforest Book,* Living Planet Press, 1990, p. 24.

246. Scott Lewis, *The Rainforest Book,* Living Planet Press, 1990, p. 24.

247. Scott Lewis, *The Rainforest Book,* Living Planet Press, 1990, p. 25.

248. Scott Lewis, *The Rainforest Book,* Living Planet Press, 1990, p. 25.

249. Scott Lewis, *The Rainforest Book,* Living Planet Press, 1990, pp. 26-27.

250. Joseph Wallace, *Sierra Magazine,* July/August, 1991, pp. 37-41.

251. Taken from a fact-sheet of Rainforest Action Network, 450 Sansome, suite 700, San Francisco, CA 94111.

252. William F. Alman, *US News & World Report,* October 31, 1988, p. 65.

253. From a fact sheet put out by the United Nations Food and Agriculture Organization.

254. William F. Alman, *US News & World Report,* October 31, 1988, p. 65.

255. Taken from a fact-sheet of Rainforest Action Network, 450 Sansome, suite 700, San Francisco, CA 94111.

256. Edward O. Wilson, *Scientific American,* September, 1989, pp. 108-116.

257. The World Wildlife Fund, *Atlas of The Environment,* Prentice Hall Press, 1990, pp. 65-68.

258. Edward O. Wilson, *Scientific American,* September, 1989, pp. 108-116.

259. Scott Lewis, *The Rainforest Book,* Living Planet Press, 1990, p. 41.

260. John Robbins, *Diet for a New America,* Stillpoint, 1987, p. 363.

261. Scott Lewis, *The Rainforest Book,* Living Planet Press, 1990, p. 42.

262. Scott Lewis, *The Rainforest Book,* Living Planet Press, 1990, p. 44.

263. Scott Lewis, *The Rainforest Book,* Living Planet Press, 1990, p. 50.

264. The World Wildlife Fund, *Atlas of The Environment,* Prentice Hall Press, 1990, pp. 65-68.

265. Michael Renner et al, Worldwatch, *State of the World 1991,* W.W. Norton & Company, 1991, p. 152.

CHAPTER ELEVEN

THE CHOICE FOR PEACE

266. Michael Renner et. al., Worldwatch, *State of the World 1991,* W.W. Norton & Company, 1991, p. 141.

267. Michael Renner et. al., Worldwatch, *State of the World 1991,* W.W. Norton & Company, 1991, p. 141.

268. Michael Renner et. al., Worldwatch, *State of the World 1991,* W.W. Norton & Company, 1991, p. 141.

269. Michael Renner et. al., Worldwatch, *State of the World 1991,* W.W. Norton & Company, 1991, p. 145.

270. Michael Renner et. al., Worldwatch, *State of the World 1991,* W.W. Norton & Company, 1991, p. 134.

271. Armed force energy use from Center for Disarmament, *The Relationship Between Disarmament and Development;* comparison with Japanese oil consumption from British Petroleum (BP), *BP Statistical Review of World Energy,* London, 1990.

272. Michael Renner et. al., Worldwatch, *State of the World 1991,* W.W. Norton & Company, 1991, p. 133.

273. Michael Renner et. al., Worldwatch, *State of the World 1991,* W.W. Norton & Company, 1991, p. 139.

274. Michael Renner et. al., Worldwatch, *State of the World 1991,* W.W. Norton & Company, 1991, p. 159.

275. Extrapolated from World Bank statistics in 1992.

276. Taken from a 1994 fact sheet of Center For Defense Information, 1500 Massachusetts Ave., N.W., Washington, DC 20005.

277. Common Agenda Coalition, *Fact Sheet Number 3,* Boston, Mass., March, 1993.

278. Michael Renner et. al., Worldwatch, *State of the World 1991,* W.W. Norton & Company, 1991, p. 159.

CHAPTER TWELVE
THE CHOICE TO BE A WARRIOR FOR THE EARTH

279. *Students Shopping for a Better World,* by the Council on Economic Priorities, 1992, p. 8.

280. Patricia Hausman, *Jack Sprat's Legacy,* Richard Marek, 1981, pp. 16-17 and 25-39,

281. John Robbins, *Diet for a New America,* Stillpoint, 1987, p. 171.

282. John Robbins, *Diet for a New America,* Stillpoint, 1987, p. 171.

283. John Robbins, *Diet for a New America,* Stillpoint, 1987, pp. 129 and 235.

284. Nathaniel Roeg, *Big Noise Magazine,* Winter, 1993, p. 8.

285. Nathaniel Roeg, *Big Noise Magazine,* Winter, 1993, p. 8.

286. Nathaniel Roeg, *Big Noise Magazine,* Winter, 1993, p. 9.

287. Louis Freedberg, *San Francisco Chronicle,* January 8, 1993, p. 3A.

INDEX

About the Authors

Ocean Robbins, age 20

Ocean started changing the world at a young age. At ages 10 and 11, he performed in four productions of the musical "Peace Child." Soon after, he started and ran "Ocean's Bakery," selling natural baked goods door-to-door to hundreds of customers around the neighborhood. At 14, he traveled to the U.S.S.R. for two international youth summits focused on the environment, meeting Mrs. Gorbachev and numerous Ambassadors and U.S. Senators to discuss environmental concerns. Ocean was co-founder with Ryan Eliason of both Creating Our Future Tour and YES!. To date, Ocean has personally spoken to more than 150,000 students in 400 schools about environmental issues, as well as facilitating camps and workshops in six countries. Ocean also travels the U.S. spreading a message of hope and inspiration to conferences, companies, and organizations. He is the Director of YES!, and is on the Board of Directors for Friends of the Earth and EarthSave.

About the Authors

Sol Solomon, age 21

Formerly from Los Angeles, Sol is now most likely somewhere on top of a mountain, snow boarding, tending a garden, or jamming on his guitar. As a founding member of Youth for Environmental Sanity (YES!) and the Granby Wilderness Society, he can also be found in action, trying to save the remaining pristine ecosystems of our planet. In high school, Sol started *The Green Republic*, an environmental club that spread to many southern California schools, and he also co-stared in the award-winning environmental documentary "Power to Survive." Since 1990, he has organized and facilitated numerous summer camps and weekend workshops that have touched and inspired the lives of thousands of young people across North America.

With his first name pronounced like the Spanish word for "sun," Sol's friends know him as someone who radiates enthusiasm. Recently, he has joined a bunch of talented musicians, forming a band that spreads a message of joy and action through music.

Ask your store to carry these books, or you may order directly from:

The Book Publishing Company
P.O. Box 99
Summertown, TN 38483

Or call: 1-800-695-2241
Please add $2.00 per book for
shipping

Vegan Cookbooks (egg- and dairy-free):

Almost No-Fat Cookbook	10.95
Burgers 'n Fries 'n Cinnamon Buns	6.95
Cookin' Healthy with One Foot Out the Door	8.95
Cooking with Gluten and Seitan	7.95
Ecological Cooking: Recipes to Save the Planet	10.95
Fabulous Beans	9.95
Instead of Chicken, Instead of Turkey:	9.95
Judy Brown's Guide to Natural Foods Cooking	10.95
New Farm Vegetarian Cookbook	8.95
Now & Zen Epicure	17.95
Physician's Slimming Guide, Neal D. Barnard, M..D	5.95
Also by Dr. Barnard:	
Power of Your Plate	11.95
Live Longer, Live Better (90 min. cassette)	9.95
Beyond Animal Experiments (90 min. cassette)	9.95
Shoshoni Cookbook	12.95
Simply Heavenly	19.95
The Sprout Garden	8.95
Ten Talents (Vegan Cookbook)	18.95
Tofu Cookery	14.95
Tofu Quick & Easy	7.95
TVP Cookbook	6.95
Vegetarian Cooking for People with Diabetes	10.95

Environment and Animal Rights:

A Vogt for the Environment	6.95
Climate in Crisis	11.95
Least Toxic Home Pest Control	8.95
Nature's Chicken	5.95
No Immediate Danger	11.95
Shepherd's Purse: Organic Pest Control	9.95
Shopping Guide for Caring Consumers	6.95
"We're All Animals" Coloring Book	3.95